Fun, Cheap, and Easy

OHIO HISTORY AND CULTURE

FRANCES McGOVERN

Fun, Cheap, and Easy

My Life in Ohio Politics, 1949–1964

THE UNIVERSITY OF AKRON PRESS

To my nephews, Mitchell, Jan, and Beirne Konarski,
and my niece, Michele Clifton.

All inquiries and permissions requests should be addressed to the
publisher, The University of Akron Press, Akron, OH 44325-1703
Manufactured in the United States of America
First edition 2002

05 04 03 02 5 4 3 2 1

LIBRARY OF CONGRESS CATALOGING-IN-PUBLICATION DATA
McGovern, Frances, 1927–
   Fun, cheap, and easy : my life in Ohio politics, 1949–1964 /
Frances McGovern. — 1st ed.
      p.   cm. — (Series on Ohio history and culture)
   Includes index.
   ISBN 1-884836-79-8 (cloth : alk. paper)
   1. McGovern, Frances, 1927– .   2. Women legislators—Ohio—
Biography.   3. Legislators—Ohio—Biography.   4. Ohio. General
Assembly. House of Representatives—Biography.   5. Ohio—
Politics and government—1951– .   6. Akron (Ohio)—Politics and
government—20th century.   I. Title.   II. Series.
F496.4.M33 A3   2001
328.771'092—dc21
2001004908

Manufactured in the United States of America
The paper used in this publication meets the minimum requirements of American National Standard for Information Sciences—
Permanence of Paper for Printed Library Materials, ANSI Z39.48—
1984.

Contents

List of Illustrations

Acknowledgments

I gratefully acknowledge the suggestion by Elton Glaser, now retired as director of The University of Akron Press, that I try my hand at writing these recollections. I also thank my patient readers, Cue and Helen Fleming, for their generous laughs, Art and Helen Louise Cullison for well-informed reviews of first drafts, and many friends and the reference librarians at the Akron-Summit County Public Library who helped fill out my memories. Above all, I thank Elton Glaser and my great friends, Margaret Oechsner and Mary Alice DeHaven, for helpful comments and those longed-for words of praise, chapter after chapter, that kept me going.

Preface

Our family often had Shredded Wheat for breakfast when I was growing up. One of my early triumphs was the realization that "Nabisco" was short for National Biscuit Company, but a bigger mystery tantalized me. Many will recall that both sides of the Shredded Wheat box used to have a picture of Niagara Falls with a small picture of the box itself in the foreground. And, of course, the small picture of the box also had a picture of the box which had a still smaller picture of the box. I knew that if I could just see better there would be boxes on boxes to infinity, but not even a magnifying glass let me see that far ahead.

It was the same way with my life. I could see the years ahead of me as I went through St. Sebastian's Grade School and then Buchtel High School. When I went on to The University of Akron, I could also see Western Reserve University Law School coming next. Beyond that, my life seemed to stretch to infinity, but I couldn't see what it held. I had some idea of being a corporation lawyer, and that's what I eventually became, but I never guessed that fifteen wonderful years in local and state politics would intervene.

Observing recent political campaigns, some of them nasty and all of them expensive, I got to remembering those years, beginning in 1949 and ending in 1964, when politics was fun, cheap, and easy. Times have changed so much since then that a history of those days seems hardly credible now, although many of you reading this will have known some of the people I knew and will have lived through some of the same events.

This book is written in the hope that readers today can enjoy living those old days with me in these pages, sharing my memories—sweetened a little by the passage of time—of the good times, laughs, griefs, failures, small successes, and great moments that made being in politics such a treasured experience.

Introduction

In 1949, Harry S. Truman was president of the United States, Frank J. Lausche, Democrat, a former mayor of Cleveland, was governor of Ohio, and Charles E. Slusser, Republican, was mayor of the otherwise very Democratic city of Akron. Akron's population measured the next year, was 274,605, up over 12 percent since 1940, and Akron was still growing.

Akron was also still a rubber town. Most of us who lived here were connected directly or indirectly with the rubber industry, and the rubber industry was woven into all our lives from childhood on. I remember we could form Red Rover teams at St. Sebastian's Grade School by rubber company affiliations. Mine was with Goodyear. My father was manager of technical service at Goodyear Plant Two. Even our six-toed cat bore the brand. It was named "Wingfoot" after Goodyear's logo.

Probably events were moving under the surface, but Akron looked the same to me in 1949 as it had looked as far back as I could remember. I had lived in the same house from the time I was born in 1927. We went to the same church and, just as religiously, to the same stores—even the same greenhouse every spring to buy our geraniums. The factories looked the same as they always had, and so did downtown where we shopped at the Holy Trinity—O'Neil's, Polsky's, and Yeager's department stores.

Downtown was anchored at one end by O'Neil's, Polsky's, and a splendid Mayflower Hotel, and at the other end by Yeager's, a string of dime stores, and the fading glory of the Portage Hotel. In between were the Flatiron Building, Quaker Oats's big factory on Howard Street, the First National Tower, Akron Savings and Loan, the Second National Building, and the YMCA and YWCA. The Ys were busy with a variety of programs, although the only ones preoccupied with fitness back then were boys reading the Charles Atlas ads on the backs of comic books. What with the Depression and World War II, there were only four new buildings in all of downtown— for Akron Furniture, Scott's dime store, WADC, and Walgreen's.

Akron's old canal ran unnoticed behind the back doors of downtown buildings until it dropped in a roar over a broken lock beside Billow's Funeral Chapel at the bottom of Ash Street hill. Akron Transportation Company's orange buses with their noxious black exhaust all funneled through downtown, as did some trolley buses swooping to the curb on the old streetcar routes. We expected a bus strike every April 1 and planned accordingly. Pigeons, living on the bounty of Quaker Oats, strutted the downtown streets by day and roosted in huge flocks under the Bowery Street bridge at night.

There were four first-run theaters: Loew's, the Colonial, the Strand, and the Palace. The Colonial was an old theater with posts we had to avoid in choosing our seats. It once brought vaudeville and road companies to town. Our parents remembered that, but I saw my first movie there in 1933 when I was six years old—*Bright Eyes* with Shirley Temple. In 1949, we listened to WADC, WAKR, and WHKK on the radio and the big swing bands on the jukeboxes at neighborhood restaurants like Hull's and Garver's. The big bands that used to come to the Palace were gone by then, however, lost to World War II and the postwar economy.

The downtown restaurants ranged all the way from Kewpie's and the Wahoo Bar and Grille through Kaase's, Clark's, Kraker's Old Heidelberg, the Garden Grille, and Stone's Grille. At Highland Square people hung out at the Bucket Shop and the Bubble Bar.

There was no expressway and, of course, no Innerbelt, and East Market still told its history in big old houses of an earlier day, many converted to funeral homes and storefronts. One storefront I enjoy remembering had a sign that read "Ed Day, The Genial Clothes Bandit."

A new train station was under construction in 1949, but we were still using Akron's old 1891 train depot below the bridge on East Market Street. That's where we got on the B&O to go to Washington. We went to Hudson to pick up the New York Central if we wanted to go to New York. The University of Akron, still a municipal university and still overcrowded with postwar enrollment under the GI Bill, was only just then starting to shoehorn some new buildings onto the little campus of 1870 between Buchtel Avenue and Carroll Street.

The Armory at High and Bowery, with a doughboy statue in the front yard, was our community center. It might be home to wrestling one night and a Tuesday Musical Society concert the next. The Akron Art Institute's Rubber Ball was held there, with music by Denny Thompson's Orchestra. Across the street, the old police building was beside the Municipal Building. Anyone trying to avoid the steep climb from Main Street to the courthouse on High Street might take an elevator halfway up the Second National Building, cross the alley behind it, and then take another elevator up to High Street from the basement of the police station or the Municipal Building. A little girl ran the clunky old elevator in the police station. "Up?" she would ask the people she picked up in the basement. They always said yes.

An old county jail like a creneleted castle stood beside the courthouse on High Street, backed by the sheriff's stone house with a big front porch facing Broadway. Lawyers and other visitors to the jail would enter between the house and the jail through a screen door into an anteroom with a linoleum floor and spittoons. The courthouse and its annex behind it had the courtrooms of all the county's six judges of the court of common pleas; Judges Emmons, Harvey, Wanamaker, Watters, Colopy, and Roetzel, the probate judge, Judge Zurz, and the Ninth District Court of Appeals with Judges Stevens, Doyle, and Hunsicker.

Except for the sheriff and maybe the coroner, all the county officials were also in the courthouse and annex, and back then there was room left over for the county law library and the Board of Elections. The officeholders, 100 percent Democratic, were, like almost everything else in Akron, the same for years. Several of them had been elected with Roosevelt in his first or second victories. Alva Russell was the prosecutor, assisted by Jackson Morris, Al Vuillemin, and Gil Hartz who were just as well known. The treasurer was Charlie Frank, the auditor was C. L. "Kelley" Bower. Frank Kroeger was recorder; Verne Bender, the clerk of courts; Dr. Amos, the coroner; Bob

Smith, the sheriff; and Art Ranney, the county engineer. The three county commissioners—this was long before Summit County's charter—were Ralph Kibler, John Poda, and Oren Carter.

Politics governed the courthouse, but not political issues. The only county issue I can remember was, perennially, some railing by the other county officeholders at Auditor Kelley Bower's practice of underestimating county revenues to keep their budgets in check. The big city issue was fluoridation of the water supply.

If we talked about national politics at all back then, it was mostly about the witch-hunts for Communists that came to be labeled McCarthyism after Senator Joe McCarthy fueled the flames with a list of so-called Communists in the State Department in February 1950. The witch-hunts stirred up many a discussion over whether ends justified means, but, while many felt the accusations and blacklists were unfair or went too far, we weren't venturing protests. Once I had lunch in the crowded cafeteria at the YWCA, and, looking around for a place to put my tray down, I asked a woman if I could sit at her table. She said yes, but when I introduced myself, she said, "I'm Thelma Furry. You may prefer to eat with someone else." Thelma Furry, a lawyer, was Akron's best-known Communist. I said I would stay. So fraught with menace were the times that I thought this was an act of courage.

If times were changing in Akron and elsewhere in 1949, I didn't notice it. I was twenty-two, unreflectingly ready to start life as an adult. My friends were finishing college. I was finishing law school after picking up three years of school by skipping a couple of years and going to summer school. The major event of our lives, World War II, was behind us. We stepped out into a world that existed rather than moved.

One How I Got into Politics

I wasn't having much luck getting a job after I got out of law school in 1949 and learned in August that I had passed the bar examination. There was no good reason to feel my being a woman was making it hard. All the same, I decided I might do better at First Federal Savings and Loan, where Geraldine Braley was president and all the employees were women.

Miss Braley got right down to business. "Do you drink?" she asked me.

"Yes," I said, "but only socially."

"My girls don't drink," she said. "Do you smoke?"

"Yes," I said again, "but I wouldn't need to smoke at work."

"Our girls don't smoke," she said. "Do you drink coffee?" she asked.

Now really, I thought. Surely that was acceptable. "Yes," I said.

"Our girls drink tea," she said. I knew the interview was over, although I don't remember when it actually ended.

It wasn't long after that that I had an appointment with Clarence Motz, the head of the law firm of Motz, Morris, Wilson, and Quine, which had its offices on the seventeenth floor of the First National Tower in downtown Akron. Clarence Motz was also the Summit County Democratic chairman. My father was a Democratic precinct committeeman, a job he regarded as a form of entertainment, but there was a factional battle going on for control of the party, and my father's dependable vote for Mr. Motz as party chairman probably explains why Mr. Motz was willing to see me. He didn't have an opening for a lawyer, but after we talked awhile, he said he needed someone to hold down the Democratic campaign headquarters until the election in November—to be there if someone came in and to answer the phone and do a few letters for Bernie Rosen, the campaign chairman. He asked if I typed. I had sworn that I would never answer yes to that question. I said "Just hunt and peck." But that was enough. "No" probably would have done just as well. The job was mine for six or seven weeks at twenty-five dollars a week. I wasn't going to get rich, but I certainly was going to enjoy myself.

Clarence E. Motz, Summit County Democratic Chairman.

The headquarters was in a loft over Ted Boyer's Backstage Bar behind the Colonial Theater on Mill Street. (I gave my mother the street address on High Street.) Mostly it was a big empty space and surprisingly clean, although the wooden floor was black with age and the walls had what was probably their original coat of paint. I sat behind a high counter at the top of the stairs that came up from the street. The office for Bernie Rosen was partitioned off behind me.

A good-sized room was also partitioned off along the front wall. I didn't hear a sound from the room the first day or two that I was there, but the next day the smell of coffee brought out a big, pleasant woman in a flowered wrapper who identified herself as a friend of Mr. Boyer's. We visited nearly every morning and usually had the place to ourselves. If someone did start to come in, there was plenty of warning on the wooden steps to send my friend skedaddling with excited hoots for her room. She had endless questions about my life and times. I regret now that I didn't ask many back because I bet she had some great stories.

Most of the time, however, I sat alone, waiting for the phone to ring and arranging and rearranging the candidates' literature along the length of the counter—"literature," I learned, being the term for campaign brochures, cards, and folders. The party's folder about all its candidates was distinguished as the "party piece."

I swept the floor every day, sure that some of the blackness would come up if I kept at it. I also set the rental chairs in rows for the occasional meeting on the premises. The high spots were the days Bernie Rosen came in. Bernie was a young lawyer and the new father of Freda, his first child. Bright and funny himself, Bernie was often amused by others. I've enjoyed his appreciative laughs all these years since, even when I've been the one amusing him. Fortunately, he didn't try to dictate a letter to me because it might have turned out written in early Greek, but sometimes he'd ask me to write to someone about something. With time on my hands and a great eagerness to please, I would then devote hours to composing a letter confirming an appointment, say, or giving notice of a meeting of the Third Ward Democratic Club.

Most ward clubs were mushroom clubs, like our own Fourth Ward club, that sprang up only at election time each year to put on a card party, a rally, or a covered-dish supper so candidates would have an opportunity to do a little campaigning. I wasn't expected to go to those meetings, but Mr. Motz (I never called him Clarence) suggested I go one Saturday to the October meeting of the Federated Democratic Women of Summit County, whose members he counted on to address all the party literature destined for the mail. There was a nice, clean division of labor between the sexes in those days. Women did the work. Men did the talking. Men also held all the public offices, with a few notable exceptions.

One of those exceptions was the speaker for the Federated Democratic Women that Saturday in the pine-paneled dining room on the first floor of the YWCA. It was State Senator Catherine R. Dobbs. Catherine Dobbs had quite a romantic story. It was said that her husband, Roy, who was mayor of Barberton at one time and somewhat older than Catherine, had educated her, albeit narrowly, and she was reputed to be a writer and a historian, although no one I knew ever saw anything she wrote. Catherine was a good-looking woman, a natural ash blonde who pulled her hair back dramatically under a black tam and who wore a black pinstriped suit and a white satin blouse that day and every other time I ever saw her, for years.

That day in October 1949, she was talking about the suffering of our boys at Valley Forge. "You can forget the food but send us shoes," she said they wrote to their families. This made a big impression on me. So did her reference to "that mute symbol standing in the corner." I sneaked a look over my shoulder. It was a dispirited flag. Catherine could be a spellbinder.

Catherine was even better known for her imagination. I don't think she ever went to a campaign event without saying it was her third or fourth meeting of the day. This wasn't a lie by her lights, just a little story. One time at a picnic, Catherine regaled our table with an account of a writers' convention she went to where she told "Ernest" about something she was writing and "Ernest" gave her some encouraging words. Not wishing to get her in any deeper, we didn't ask who Ernest was.

The visitors I enjoyed most at the Backstage Bar headquarters were the ward leaders. I still fondly remember Lemmon Gill, Johnnie Fivecoat, Otto Rasche, John Stadler, Joan Fleenor, S. S. Phillips, Harry Orr, and George

State Senator Catherine R. Dobbs, 1954 campaign photo.

Spikerman. My favorite was Otto Rasche, the Third Ward leader, a tall, iras-
cible man who was getting on in years but who sprang up the steps to the
headquarters like a youngster and often brought flowers from his garden.

I considered myself an old pro when I learned the boundaries of the
wards and could locate references such as to the Seventh Ward (Firestone
Park), the Ninth (Kenmore), or the First (North Hill). The ward candidates
for city council I knew better from their brochures than from acquaintance.
Chick Madden, Ed Erickson, Ed Flowers, Francis Greissing, Paul Bixler, John
Head, Leo Laney, and Leo Berg were our candidates in eight of Akron's ten
wards. The Republican incumbents, lawyers Kenneth Baker in the Fourth
Ward and Howard C. Walker in the Eighth Ward, were too formidable to
make our Democratic candidates memorable. Ralph Turner and two other
Democrats were running for council-at-large. Ralph won, but the other two
winners were Republicans—Russell Bird, who had been councilman from
the Sixth Ward and was later mayor of Akron and sheriff of Summit County,
and Charlie Burns, the manager of the Elks Club. Bill Victor was running for
his first term as a municipal judge that year.

The head of the ticket was Richard W. Tobin, a portly Irishman more
than good enough to take on the incumbent mayor, Charles E. Slusser, but
not always ready to do so. I tried writing something for Dick that I heard
about the industrial relations program of Michael V. DiSalle, then the popular mayor of Toledo, but I don't recall that it was used.

The end of the campaign brought a great letdown. Not only had politics
got in my blood, but I hated to start job-hunting again. Clarence Motz came
up with an answer. He suggested I open my own office in Barberton, and he
offered to lend me the money to do so. He got started in Cuyahoga Falls,
he said, and ever afterward drew business from the Falls. Maybe I would
have the same luck starting in Barberton, and he would see if maybe there
wouldn't be an opening for me in Akron before too long. So I went to Barberton, borrowing, all told, $700 the first year and repaying it in painful
$100 chunks the second year. The third year, I joined Mr. Motz's firm.

Two Learning the Ropes

My life as a lawyer started very slowly, but I was soon deeper in politics. Mr. Motz saw to that. He was given to repeating my name in a considering way. No wonder. An archrival in the factional battle within the local party (Regulars vs. Roosters) was Mary McGowan, the queen of the Rooster Club. Mary held the position of Democratic state central committeewoman for our congressional district—a source of great embarrassment to the Regulars. It didn't help that the state central committeeman, Tony Lombardi, was also from the Rooster Club.

"Frances McGovern," Mr. Motz said again one day. "It isn't by any chance Mary Frances, is it?" I was sorry to disappoint him. My name is Pauline Frances. Nevertheless, he had the great idea that voters might get Mary McGowan and Frances McGovern mixed up on the ballot if I ran against Mary in 1950 for state central committeewoman. I agreed to run so quickly that Mr. Motz evidently felt a moment's compunction and warned me not to say yes without thought. "Once you start running for office, you never get out of politics," he told me. He was almost right. Fifteen years later, I did get out of politics but, oh, it was hard to do.

The Rooster Club was named for the rooster that used to be on the top of the ballot, along with an eagle, in the days before the Massachusetts ballot was adopted in Ohio. Anyone wanting to vote a straight ticket could simply put an *X* under the rooster to vote for all Democrats or under the eagle to vote for all Republicans. The Rooster Club was run by a triumvirate— Walter "Buck" Coyle, Tony Lombardi, and Harry Van Berg. Tony and Harry were lawyers and later were judges. Buck Coyle was a former newspaperman at the old *Akron Times-Press,* which had been taken over by the *Akron Beacon Journal* years before. He ran a popular ice cream parlor with his wife, Mary Coyle, first in a store built on the front of the historic Howe house on East Exchange Street across from the *Beacon* and then at Highland Square.

I liked all three of the Rooster Club leaders, particularly Mr. Coyle, who was the father of Joann, Colleen, Larry, Terry, and Tim, with whom I had gone to school at St. Sebastian's. In fact, Colleen was in my class and a friend. But loyalty runs in a straight line in politics. That meant the leaders of the Rooster Club had to be treated as mortal enemies by the faithful Regulars. Judge Vincent Zurz of the probate court, the only Rooster Club officeholder, also had to be treated as an enemy since he had a fair amount of patronage to distribute, all of which went unfailingly to the Rooster Club ranks. Mary McGowan was Judge Zurz's court reporter, and she took notes with dramatic flourishes and incredible speed when needed. This wasn't often, however, in that court, so she didn't get much practice. Lawyers who needed an accurate record of proceedings brought their own reporters.

One good thing about running for the state central committee was that it was cheap. I needed only a little money for gasoline, raffle tickets, and inexpensive door prizes. I bought some fingertip towels on sale and wrapped them nicely, with my card on top. John Stadler, running against state central committeeman Tony Lombardi, shared the hand card with me. My picture on the card didn't altogether satisfy Mr. Motz—he favored a direct look and a good smile—but I liked it. It was a graduation photograph with a dreamy

Mary McGowan, 1964 campaign photo.

Anthony L. Lombardi, 1964 campaign photo.

Hand card for 1950 Democratic State Central Committee election.

gaze and no glasses taken by Paul Esselburn, who glamorized all his sitters. But the text was businesslike. It said I was a practicing attorney, a graduate of The University of Akron and Western Reserve University Law School, and active in civic affairs.

I got in trouble at my first meeting as a candidate, a First Ward card party at the Carovillese Hall on North Hill. Lemmon Gill, the ward leader, a bailiff for Judge Roetzel in the domestic relations court, introduced all the candidates and brought me forward like the bride at a wedding. The next morning I got a call from Mr. Motz. "I hear you won the raffle last night," he said. Yes, I did, I said happily—a very nice toaster! "Candidates aren't supposed to take prizes," he told me. "Ah," I said. "I see." That taught me an important rule of etiquette for candidates: buy the prizes, buy the chances on the prizes, and, with a grand gesture, ask that one's winning chances be redrawn. This was to everyone's advantage: the people whose votes we were seeking got the prizes, the candidates who bought enough chances got several opportunities to ingratiate themselves by showing their generosity, and the club got the revenue from selling the chances. I couldn't help wondering who had hastened to inform Mr. Motz about the toaster, but another rule for candidates was "Always forward."

Almost immediately, I got into trouble again, but not of my own volition. My mother, who had no feel for politics, had known Mary McGowan for years. In fact, Mary was an older cousin of a friend of Mother's who had been Mother's maid of honor many years earlier. Worse still, Mary lived only a short distance from our house, on the corner of Moreley and Copley Roads, and she didn't drive. When Mother realized that Mary and I were sometimes going to the same meetings, she felt I should pick Mary up and bring her along with me. I protested that not only was I running against Mary, but she always had someone who could drive her to meetings. Margaret Head, for one, wife of the Seventh Ward councilman, frequently took her around. But since I needed to drive the family car, Mother prevailed. I hoped Mary would just thank me for offering to take her, but she accepted.

I probably only drove Mary to two or three meetings, but for me they were memorable. It was not as if I were making any headway. I had no idea what a state central committeewoman did (actually nothing but choose the state chairman), but I would get up when introduced and say earnestly that I had the right kind of education and the right kind of experience to do a good job. That was my line, and I stuck to it. Mary had a better line. Red hair flaming with Celtic henna, Mary would say, "Well, one thing for sure. There's going to be an Irishwoman elected. Thanks for your vote!" Even I had to laugh. She wiped me out at every meeting.

The Fourteenth Congressional District, in which we were running for the state central committee, was much larger in 1950 than it is today. It included Portage, Medina, and Lorain Counties, as well as Akron's Summit County. Medina had too few Democratic voters to be worth any effort, but Mr. Motz himself took John Stadler and me to meet the Democratic chairmen of Portage and Lorain Counties. The Portage County chairman was a lawyer who plainly got no advantage from his political position. His office in

Kent was at the top of an open staircase, and there were dusty papers, files, and books on the floor and all over the place. The walls, which had a kind of oatmeal wallpaper, as I recall it, were hung with old calendars that had aged and curled in place. A bed was half-hidden behind a bookcase.

The Democratic chairman of Lorain County, Joe Uhaly, was more prosperous, judging by his office, and he was willing to help. But Mr. Motz thought some extra help would be useful, and, knowing the population of Lorain was heavily ethnic, he enlisted a well-known Akronite, John Mihaly, to introduce us to that population one warm spring day. John Stadler and I remember that day still with disbelieving laughs whenever we run into each other.

We went together in John Mihaly's car, joined by Catherine Turner, Ralph Turner's wife, who was vice-chairman of the Summit County Democratic Party. For that day, she was acting as our chaperone since I was young and traveling with two men. A chaperone, of course, wasn't really necessary except to reflect the proprieties of the period. John Stadler was handsome enough, but he was happily married, and John Mihaly was unbelievably homely, a big snaggletoothed man with a bald head that came to a point and a Tatar slant to his eyes that suggested cunning. His looks didn't serve him well. He was more than ordinarily intelligent and was outgoing and generous, but it took me a long while to appreciate his virtues, because my first impression had been formed by watching him eat apple slices off the blade of his penknife. He was a public accountant in the part of South Akron known as Goosetown, and he was running for the Ohio Senate in a district that overlapped the congressional district.

Off we went about two in the afternoon, with John Mihaly driving. To our surprise, John turned south, away from Lorain. After we picked up a stout but flashy girlfriend in Canton and made several stops at gas stations to leave boxes of John's campaign matches, we resumed our trip to Lorain, but by late afternoon we had only got as far as Peninsula, six miles from Akron, and by then we needed refreshment. I had an ice cream cone, eaten in the middle of Peninsula's main street, Peninsula not then being a town encumbered with much traffic. Catherine Turner stayed in the car, stiff with disapproval of Mihaly's friend. Catherine had a Scot's burr I loved to hear, but she had little to say on this trip. Her eyes bored into the back of Mihaly's head when he got back in the driver's seat. By then the sun was nearly gone, and there were a few flakes of snow in the air.

We got to Lorain about ten o'clock that night in a snowstorm. Our destination was a bar and club where John knew the bartender and the patrons who had braved the bad weather. He introduced us to all. We sat over some beer. And then we turned around and left for home. Only the cards we left behind and John's matches evidenced that we had ever seen Lorain.

Were the voters confused between McGovern and McGowan when election day came? Maybe in the other counties, but not in Summit County, where most of the votes were cast for party offices in the primary. Mary McGowan and Tony Lombardi won reelection with big majorities. I knew enough about high school and college elections to know what I should do. On my next trip to the courthouse, I went to the probate court and congratulated Mary. Mary was her usual gracious self. "I would have beaten you by a lot more if I hadn't been so busy working on Judge Zurz's campaign," she said.

Three **Apprentice**

Defeat didn't end my political career. Mr. Motz was sure I would be good for something someday. Meanwhile, he thought I could learn from the elders of the party at their regular meetings, provided I listened and didn't speak. I'm a great talker, so that came hard for me, but I managed to listen for nearly five years. The elders were sage and seasoned pros: Akron's ten Democratic ward leaders and the so-called country leaders of the suburbs and townships. They didn't so much decide issues—Mr. Motz seldom presented any—as offer opinions and counsel. These were received with complete attention, no matter how views differed. And differ they did, because no two members of the group were alike except in their consuming interest in party politics, an interest seldom shared by officeholders and candidates. There were only a couple of people in the group who raised money, and the members weren't showy, but they were uniquely useful in recruiting good, loyal committeemen who could be counted on to reelect the party leadership and to get out the literature and the vote at campaign time. Sometimes they would also identify good potential candidates for ward contests.

Inevitably, I had some favorites: Otto Rasche, the Third Ward leader who had brought flowers to the old Backstage Bar headquarters; Johnny Fivecoat, the Second Ward leader, whom I took to be Irish because he looked like a leprechaun and was a born contrarian; Joe Orr, a tool and die maker with a big family who succeeded his uncle Harry Orr as Seventh Ward leader when Harry died; Louis Assmus from Sagamore Hills Township, a round man with a round face and a sweet smile who never had anything bad to say about anyone; and George Fisher from Boston Township, whom I celebrate memorially from time to time with a "Grandpa George" hamburger at Fisher's Restaurant in Peninsula, which he started and which is now run by one of his grandchildren.

I also liked all the women—three of them in the twenty or so members of the group. Joan Fleenor, the Fifth Ward leader who ran a lunch counter on

East Exchange Street near Main, had a tough manner but warmed up instantly when given any kind word or praise. Margaret Eubanks, from Coventry Township, was girlishly pretty, so her sharp tongue sometimes took people by surprise, but I always enjoyed it. My special friend was Catherine Turner, the county chairwoman, appointed, she said, by Mr. Motz to "look after" me.

The most important members were the Democratic members of the Summit County Board of Elections, E. E. Leonard and Walter J. Scheu. (E. E. Brown and Ray Bliss were the two Republican members.) Two better lieutenants than Ernie Leonard and Wally Scheu could not have been chosen. Ernie was the more professional, and by all accounts he was a better shot than Mr. Motz when picking off turtles in a millpond owned by Mr. Motz on State Route 8 at Graham Road. Ernie and his wife Adeline lived in the farmhouse beside the pond. Wally, with a mild, sweet manner, was better at recruiting precinct committeemen and keeping them loyal. He gave the impression of being absentminded, but he knew all the election deadlines, and I don't think he ever forgot a birthday or missed the funeral of a loyal supporter.

The meetings were in Ernie Leonard's and Wally Scheu's office at the Board of Elections in the basement of the courthouse, a long, narrow room with a high ceiling located behind the elevators. I always sat near the middle, across from a picture hanging over Ernie's desk of his army unit in the war. World War I, that was. World War II was not yet represented in the leadership except by Bernie Rosen from time to time. I was probably the only one in the room who found the puttees and Smokey Bear hats in Ernie's picture a little quaint. The Young Men's and Young Women's Democratic Clubs, where many of the postwar generation were to be found, were mostly preoccupied with internecine warfare, although many members worked hard on campaigns. I belonged to the Young Women's Democratic Club but followed Clarence Motz's advice to lie low and never seek any office in the club or any credit for anything lest I stir up someone's competitive juices.

What I remember best at those ward and country leaders' meetings were the discussions of candidates. "Nobody ever sees him," one would say grimly. Another complained a candidate never called him for help. Laziness was the worst fault. Cockiness was almost as bad. The greatest tribute was "He's working hard for himself." Of course, every other year there were races for precinct committeemen, and many Regulars were opposed by Rooster Club members. For these offices, only one virtue was sought: loyalty— faithful adherence to the Regulars' cause and turning up to vote at the meeting to elect the county chairman and other party officers.

John Stadler and I ran again for the state central committee in 1952 and lost again to Tony Lombardi and Mary McGowan. But, as usual, the Regulars won a majority of the precinct committee races in Summit County. That produced a meeting to elect the local party officers that was funnier than a Marx Brothers movie.

The meeting was held soon after the primary in the gymnasium of Hower Vocational High School, which is gone now but which used to face Perkins Square across from Children's Hospital. I was watching from the first row of the balcony, so I didn't miss a thing, although I was nearly carried away by laughter a couple of times as the workings of democracy were revealed.

It has to be remembered that this was the period of battles for control of the party between the Regulars, led by Mr. Motz, and the Rooster Club outsiders who were trying to get in. That doesn't mean there were any issues of principle involved. The goal on both sides, simply put, was to win offices, influence, and those opportunities to serve the public that some insensitively describe as "patronage." At the meeting in 1952 that I remember so well, Clarence Motz was on the dais as the incumbent chairman of the party. His lieutenants—Wally Scheu and Ernie Leonard, Sixth Ward leader Stan Phillips, and a couple of other party stalwarts—were in the front row, with the other Regulars behind them and across the center aisle. Tony Lombardi, Harry Van Berg, Buck Coyle, and the rest of the opposition from the Rooster Club were halfway down the aisle to Mr. Motz's left.

Mr. Motz opened the meeting by inviting nominations for the party chairmanship for the next two years. His good friend Ernie Leonard was instantly on his feet. But so was Tony Lombardi, his mortal enemy. Mr. Motz recognized Ernie, who nominated—who else?—Clarence Motz. "Are there any further nominations?" Mr. Motz asked. His eyes swept the entire room, but just above Tony Lombardi's head. "Hearing none . . . ," he went on. Agonized cries broke from the Rooster Club. Tony tried to stand on his chair. Harry Van Berg, who was much taller, waved his arms and shouted into the uproar. But his voice was lost. After a suitable interval during which Mr. Motz was unable to hear any other nominations, he recognized Wally Scheu for a motion to cast a unanimous ballot for the sole nominee. Wally quickly got to his feet and read the motion from a script. "Hearing no objection, the motion passes," Mr. Motz said smoothly.

"The next order of business," he continued, "is the nomination of the treasurer." (At least that was the next one I remember.) Party Regular Stan Phillips was recognized and he nominated the incumbent, Leo Walter. Again, Mr. Motz asked for other nominations, but there were none, although not for lack of trying. Poor Tony Lombardi, calling out hoarsely for recognition, was leaping up and down and reaching really extraordinary heights, and at least half the Rooster Club contingent was standing up and shouting. But it was Wally Scheu who was called upon again for a motion to cast a unanimous ballot for the sole nominee, and it, too, passed without objection after Mr. Motz's eyes swept the audience searchingly to determine whether there was any dissent but somehow failed to see the fistfights and the screaming, contorted faces in the aisle.

And so the meeting proceeded until all the offices were filled for the next two years by the Regulars. I don't dare examine what dark corner of my soul thought this was funny, because I have to laugh all over again when I remember it.

Four **First Run**

A great opportunity arose in 1954. At that time, Summit County had five members in the Ohio House of Representatives, all elected countywide, and two of them were not going to run for re-election: Anna F. O'Neil from Kenmore, the dean of the delegation who had served for twenty years and was chairman of the House Finance Committee when the Democrats had a majority, and Fred Harter, a highly regarded businessman and president of Harter Dairy, who was moving over from the House to the Senate. Mr. Motz once told me that Fred Harter originally approached Amos "Tiny" Engelbeck or some other leading Republican when he wanted to run for the legislature, but he got a cool reception so he went to see Mr. Motz. Mr. Motz welcomed him into the Democratic fold at once. With the same faith in names that led him to involve me in politics, Mr. Motz was confident that voters would see the virtue of anyone named Harter because Dow Harter (no relation) had been our congressman for years, George Harter had been mayor of Akron and then state representative, and later George's widow, Sophia Harter, had succeeded him.

With vacancies for two new House members, it was open season. Seventeen of us ran for the House in the Democratic primary and thirteen more in the Republican primary.

Since the party leaders were wishing me well and I had been on the ballot twice before in Democratic primaries, I felt I had a small edge. That didn't mean I was endorsed by the party in the primary—just that I was introduced early and kindly at campaign events. The party had had a bad experience with a primary endorsement in 1953, and, like the cat that stepped on a hot burner and never got near the stove again, it wasn't going to endorse again. What happened in 1953 was that the mayor of Akron, Charles E. Slusser, went to Washington as head of the Public Housing Administration under President Eisenhower and was succeeded as mayor by Russell Bird, whom the Democrats were sure they could defeat. That was, moreover, the year Warren E. Carter at last agreed to run for mayor on the Democratic ticket after years of being begged to do so. He was president of Carter-Jones Lumber Company, one of the biggest companies in town, and he was a leader in the business community. The trouble was that a longtime loyal friend of the Regulars, Tenth Ward councilman Leo Berg, had also decided to run. The party felt obliged to endorse Warren Carter, but it was Leo who won when his outraged friends, including party treasurer Leo Walter, and a delighted Rooster Club rallied around him.

Warren Carter had another little problem in that campaign. Although he was open-minded, never a racist, he had been born in Arkansas, and, at a time when "Negro" was the term preferred by the black community, "nigra" was the best pronunciation he could manage. A couple of times, Mr. Motz sent me out with him when he was campaigning. I helped him find the church basement, union hall, or ethnic club where a meeting was to be held, but my presence was also supposed to remind him to say that word right if it came up. He really tried to do so. Once he looked at me pleadingly when he failed. But he always failed.

Filing as a candidate for the Ohio House of Representatives, 1956.

I found out early in the primary that running for the House was different from running for the state central committee. For one thing, there were so many of us that campaign speeches had to be very short. Finding the right few words wasn't particularly difficult for Thomas L. Thomas, the only incumbent in the Democratic primary, because someone once told him a candidate should repeat his name at least three times and that provided Tommy with most of the content he needed. "Thank you, Mr. Chairman," he'd begin, and continue, "I am Thomas L. Thomas, your state representative. Thomas L. Thomas has done a good job for you in Columbus, and you can always count on Thomas L. Thomas. So, remember to vote for Thomas L. Thomas on election day." Tommy, always impeccably groomed and the only man I ever knew who could carry off a three-piece suit, had the name of a famous singer and the dark eyes of a Welshman, but he wasn't a singer and he wasn't Welsh. He pronounced the *Th* in "Thomas" as in "the" or "that," so it was evident he had changed his name. No one held it against him. He won time and time again.

My problem was I couldn't get up the nerve to say straight out that I was good, or even "vote for me" or "remember me." What I did, finally, was list what I thought were qualifications—education, experience, whatever—and then conclude by saying "I hope you will feel I am qualified to represent you," thus leaving the judgment to the voter. I didn't mind assertions of qualifications by others, however. I even remember greatly enjoying an assertion once. In 1958, the state Democratic Party feared a bedsheet ballot of candidates in the primary race for governor, so it created a screening committee to narrow the field. The then mayor of Columbus, Maynard Sensenbrenner, was one of the candidates. "I screened myself and found I was OK," he said. As might be expected, that ended the screening process. (I thought of that when Dick Cheney, who was screening vice presidential candidates for George W. Bush in 2000, ended up selecting himself.)

When the primary was over, I was one of the winners. In fact, I came in first. To put all the bragging in one place, I came in first in the primary and general elections every time I ran for state representative—in 1954, 1956, and 1958.

Looking back on it, I realize that those of us who had the opportunity to run for the Ohio House in the 1950s were lucky. That was before new rules engendered by the United States Supreme Court's decision in *Baker v. Carr* in 1962 required running from districts of approximately equal population. Whether I liked it personally or not, I had to agree the decision was right. The old law was unfair in that every county in Ohio was entitled to at least one vote, no matter how small its population. Vinton County, for example, with only about ten thousand people, had its own state representative. So did Monroe County, which was almost as small. Counties with greater populations were entitled to more representatives, but not proportionately. At the time I ran, Summit County was about twenty-seven times larger than Vinton County, but it had only five representatives. The largest county, Cuyahoga, had only seventeen representatives. This disproportionate representation of small counties gave rural members, known as the "Cornstalk Brigade," the ruling voice in the Ohio House.

But there was a lot to say for the old system. The carved-out districts now required to equalize the voting population are too big to be neighborhoods and too arbitrary to have any identity. Many people have difficulty in figuring out what district they are in. "The 43rd" or "44th district" doesn't run trippingly off the tongue. Also, the campaign events are nearly always fund-raisers because candidates trying to reach an amorphous constituency are practically obliged to rely on expensive ads and mailings and raise big sums of money to pay for them. Occasionally, money alone seems to control the outcome of a race. Moreover, without many campaign forums for reaching voters, some candidates resort to ugly appeals to prejudice in their efforts to attract voters' attention.

Another good thing about running at large—countywide—for five openings was that we didn't necessarily feel we were running against each other. There was a kind of camaraderie. After all, there were going to be five winners. We never attacked each other, Republican or Democrat. After the primary, the five of us who were Democratic nominees even tried to run as a team. "Get the most out of your vote. Vote for all five Democrats for the House," we would say. At least we did so at Democratic meetings. We weren't crazy, however. We knew perfectly well that, on average, people voted for only three or so candidates, and in 1954, there were three incumbents: Thomas L. Thomas, the Democrat, and Ray Souers and Ed Rowe, Republicans. We also knew that "one-shot" voting for a candidate—that is, voting for only one of the five—gave that candidate an enormous advantage. Our "vote for five" pitch was partly a pledge to each other that we weren't going to ask outside our immediate families for one-shots.

One candidate was so selfless he stands out in my memory. That was John Campbell, when he ran for state representative in the 1950s on his first try for political office. John was a stocky, curly-headed youngster who never outgrew his boyish looks even when he became a judge much later. John's father had a restaurant somewhere around South Main and Route 224, and when John had a campaign rally there at the restaurant, he not only had free food—unheard of today when even hot dogs or spaghetti dinners are priced to raise money—but he also invited all of us who were also running for state representative, and made sure each of us was introduced and had an opportunity to speak. The only good he got out of that was that we all spoke well of him, at least that night. He gave me something more: he told me one time that he passed out my literature along with his own when he went out door-to-door campaigning. Maybe I would have returned the favor if I knew of it, but I'm not sure I could have been that nice.

Despite the camaraderie among the candidates of both parties, there was a little envy of the Republican candidates among us Democrats. We had to pay something like $200 each to help defray the cost of the party piece mailed to all voters, but we heard the Republicans at the very same time were *receiving* $250 each for their campaigns. Trivial sums, one might say today, but they weren't trivial then. I can't recall exactly how much I spent in any of my campaigns for the legislature, but I'm almost sure that it was only a little over a thousand dollars, and maybe even less. That did, however, buy a lot in the 1950s: ten thousand hand cards with the union bug from Alex Eigenmacht at Exchange Printing or Clayton Herriott at Craftsman Press, two small Saturday and Monday "tombstone" ads in the *Akron Beacon Journal* just before the general election, door prizes, program ads, six fifteen-second spots on radio station WCUE in the Palace Arcade, and some limited mailings. It also bought 150 or 200 bumper stickers, depending on whether they were peelable or not. I economized with nonpeelable stickers the first time I ran but got so many wrathful complaints when the time came to remove them that I found it prudent to switch to peelable stickers the next time.

What with races every other year for five positions in that period, there were a great many candidates to remember. Some I remember for the wrong reasons. There was the professor of political science at The University of Akron, Roy Sherman, who considered himself to be uniquely qualified for public office but who spit when he talked. There was the otherwise likable real estate man, Clay Deane, who thought women liked dirty jokes, so he gave them his best at women's meetings and used his wonderfully expressive eyebrows to make sure they got the point. There was Elisabeth Buehl, an advertising executive who would have made an excellent member but who stressed out the voters with her catchy ads. One of the ads had a picture of her walking toward the camera and holding on to her hat as if in a high wind, with the cutline "Here comes Mrs. Buehl."

One tall, willowy young candidate at a meeting in Cuyahoga Falls imprinted himself forever on my memory when, evidently feeling a little breeze as he got up to speak, he discovered he was unzipped where he should have been zipped. Gesturing extravagantly with one hand, he spoke with unusual eloquence while he slowly—and he thought unobtrusively—worked his zipper up, inch by inch, with the other hand. The audience was with him all the way. I believe he was encouraged by the generous applause he got that night.

One thing we could count on was opportunity. We could find voters everywhere because we could draw on events all over the county. That meant we were always busy and always spread thin, but since we all had the same opportunities, the candidates who worked hardest usually did best. Some efforts were, however, more productive than others. I discovered that after trying to campaign door to door in Kenmore, which must have the highest number of porch steps per block of any part of Akron. I settled instead for the houses on North Hill in the Dayton Street neighborhood with short walks and only one step or two up to the front door. I got a surprisingly big vote there, and Lemmon Gill, the First Ward leader, told me he had worked extra hard on my campaign. I'm sure he did, but, to be on the safe side, I continued to go door-to-door there every time I ran.

Another effort that proved to be unproductive was "papering" cars with campaign material at the new shopping centers. Not only did people hate discovering the literature on their windshields *after* they got in their cars, but far too many of them turned out not to be county residents. The new era of regional shopping had begun.

Five **Campaigning**

I don't remember when I went to my first covered-dish supper as a candidate, but I do remember taking a big plate of food to a table and sitting down with some of the women who were putting on the dinner. "These baked beans are really good," I said. Suddenly every eye was on me, but only one of the women was smiling. "And isn't this jello salad delicious," I said quickly. That brought another smile. My praise for the macaroni and cheese was passed to someone down the table. After I complimented the corn pudding, Johnny Marzetti, and even the cottage cheese brought by some unambitious soul, I still found it politic to go back for succotash, candied yams, tuna noodle casserole, and Spanish rice. And then came the desserts. "I wonder who made this wonderful pineapple upside-down cake," I said. "And these heavenly brownies!"

I loved those dinners. Fortunately, there weren't many of them, or I would have foundered. I didn't feel the same way about chicken paprikash dinners, a Barberton specialty. The fewer of them the better, as far as I was concerned. Years later, I discovered chicken paprikash can be good—and it was Barberton chicken paprikash—but at political events, what passed for the real thing was made with old stewing hens in a watery broth.

Most people seem to remember rubber chicken or shoe leather cutlets as the entrée at the big political dinners, but I didn't think the dinners were all that bad. If they were important, like the Democrats' annual Jefferson-Jackson Day dinners and the Republicans' Lincoln Day dinners, they were held at the Sheraton Mayflower in the Grand Ballroom on the second floor, and the hotel served good food. The best part of dinners at the Mayflower was the moment when the lights were dimmed and the waiters marched into the darkened room to some stirring music with Baked Alaska flaming on trays they held over their heads. I never got tired of that drama, even when more sophisticated diners were greeting it with groans.

What was hard to take at the big dinners was the sheer length of the evenings. We knew in advance what we were in for because there were print-ed programs at every place. The invocation was over early, of course, but the rest went on and on. The Pledge of Allegiance was led by some dignitary, greetings were given at length by up to four visitors from out of town, and remarks were made by one or two more, all suitably introduced. Then came the introduction of the speaker and finally the speaker, the Honorable so-and-so. And that wasn't necessarily all. After the speech, there might be one or more of the following: a presentation, a memorial, a tribute and re-sponse, or an appreciation. Not for nothing were heads bowed for the clos-ing prayer. We were worn out.

The time was not wasted, however, by aspiring politicians. It was at din-ners like those that I learned the "man who" form of introduction, so often and so splendidly used every four years at the national party conventions. As many can recall, the recital of a speaker's attributes begins with the one doing the introduction expressing the privilege of introducing "a man who" is known to all, then going on to extoll his merits as "a man who" did such and such, "a man who" is now doing such and such, "a man who" has always done such and such, "a man who" has, moreover, held such and such a posi-tion with distinction, "a man who" has fearlessly espoused such and such, and, as the peroration approaches, "a man whose" devotion is to the com-mon man (common values at Republican gatherings). The introduction winds up on a rising note, with the speaker being "given" to the audience by his present title, his next title (if a candidate), and, after a pause equivalent to a drumroll, his full name, including initials and nickname, if any. If this is done right, the audience will be standing up with cheers and applause as the speaker rises.

In 1960, a man named George Mark who advertised himself as presi-dent of the Polish-American Veterans of America was running for Congress in the Democratic primary and sought to capitalize on the luster of the speaker being introduced at that year's Jefferson-Jackson Day dinner. He hired a brass quartet to march in and play a fanfare for the speaker, then turn and salute the audience. But John Mihaly was also a candidate for Congress that year, and John, who, as I have said, was not dumb, saw the "Mark for Congress" signs in the hatbands of the quartet when they were assembling by the elevators outside the ballroom. He and a friend grabbed one of his own signs and timed their entrance for the fanfare. When the trumpeters turned to salute the crowd, they found themselves playing to an immense "Mihaly for Congress" sign with John himself, smiling his gaptoothed smile, holding up one end.

It was at one of these dinners that I learned the value of simple declarative sentences. I learned it from John F. Kennedy in 1959 when he spoke to our local Jefferson-Jackson Day dinner. At first I wondered why he was rarely interrupted by applause. Heaven knows we were eager to clap for anything he said. Then it dawned on me. The problem was that he never gave us a good clean statement to affirm. There simply wasn't time to diagram any of his sentences to extract the content before he was on to the next one. By 1960, when he was running for president, he had learned how to elicit a response. I was in the Los Angeles Coliseum in 1960 for his speech accepting his nomination for the presidency. In the twilight, with the distant hum of a small plane overhead, in a single spotlight, his head thrown back, he said, "Give me your help. Give me your hand, your voice and your vote." Theodore White reported in *The Making of the President 1960* that each phrase brought cheers. From me, they brought an undying commitment.

Some of the most important stops during campaigns were at ethnic clubs—the Polish-American Club on Glenwood Avenue, various German and Hungarians clubs on Grant Street, and the Slovak and Slovene clubs in Barberton. I rather liked the Polish-American Club, where I was introduced in English with courtly compliments. I do remember, however, that when I got up to speak the first time and said something like "Dobry nuts" I got a big laugh. I had been told that meant either "thank you" or "Good day," but, if so, something must have been very wrong with my pronunciation. I didn't have to say anything at all to get a laugh when I went once, and only once, to the men's club at Sts. Cyril and Methodius Church in Barberton. I was introduced in an unfamiliar tongue, and just what was said about me I don't know, but whatever it was, it was so funny to the members that some had to stamp their feet and wipe their eyes before I could speak. I didn't dare say much for fear I'd set them off again. After I was elected, I also gave many program speeches to various organizations, and many times several of us legistators would appear on panels and then respond to questions.

Picnics were important in the 1950s. They filled in the otherwise thin summer schedules, and they gave candidates opportunities to meet people who would never be seen at ward meetings or other political events. There were so many picnics back then that it wasn't necessary to know who was having a picnic or when or where. On Sundays, we candidates simply went to the picnic grounds—Tomsik's, Mannerchor, Liedertafel, and others. Les Wolfe, the county engineer, gave me a map marked with all the usual sites in the southern part of the county. I always began at Tomsik's, parking my car in the dusty parking lot and making my way to the gate with grasshoppers leaping this way and that ahead of me. The gate was a card table, usually with a couple of substantial women in charge who asked whether we were members or guests. Guests paid a small admission charge—fifty cents, if I remember—and were waved in. I had a quota of five hundred hand cards (half a shoebox full) to give out every Sunday. That usually meant I went to three picnics. On gray days, I might have to go to four or five.

The lighter side of campaigning, 1956.

Each candidate had his own approach to picnickers. The important feature of mine was to keep moving because I discovered the crowd shifted every thirty minutes or so. That meant I didn't dare get into conversations or accept invitations to sit down and eat. At two of the parks, there were drinks sheds, and the men who were candidates were expected to stand a round of drinks. I was spared that, but delays were sometimes unavoidable anyway. That's when I would discover I was giving cards to the same people again—people who had moved to new positions and who didn't like my forgetting so soon that I had already met them.

Forgetfulness did help me in one regard. In a far corner of Tomsik's Park was a small, roofed pavilion where women prepared mountains of food and men played cards at tables outside under the trees. Every Sunday I finished my circuit of the park by giving my hand cards to the people in that corner. As far as I knew, they were different people every week. But on election day when my mother went to vote, she observed that a small man was passing out my cards just beyond the flags at our voting booth near Buchtel High School. She introduced herself and thanked him. His name was Green, he said, and the cards came from ones I gave him and his friends playing cards at Tomsik's every Sunday. He had gathered them up week after week all summer and now was recycling them for me.

Once at the Liedertafel or the Mannerchor grounds, the people at one table refused my cards. That is probably the hardest thing for a candidate to accept. To this day, I take perfume samples, flyers, and religious tracts without fail, remembering the embarrassment of being turned down. That day I realized why my cards were refused when one woman stood up at the end of the table and said proudly, as much to the others as to me, "I'm a citizen; I can vote," and reached out her hand for my card.

A memorable moment of a different kind came at one Sunday picnic when I was running for my third term in the House. A man said jovially, "You stick with it, Mary, and one of these days you're going to make it." I don't know whether I was more taken down a peg by his thinking I had never been elected or, considering my history, by his calling me "Mary."

When the picnic circuit ended, the fall events began to proliferate. One thing most of us candidates did for each other was pass along the word about meetings that some may not have heard about. By October, there could be as many as three meetings a night. The candidates who were introduced early had a good chance of making all of them, especially if the route lay along the north or east legs of the Akron Expressway—its only legs in the 1950s. For mysterious reasons, however, it always seemed as if meetings on the same night were far apart. Wild trips across town, such as from Barberton to Hudson or from Portage Lakes to Cuyahoga Falls, were common. One night, because of slow introductions, we arrived, one by one, too late for a meeting at a tavern far north on old Route Eight. So we had a convivial meeting of our own. But another night, when I was heading late to Twinsburg, I saw a terrible rat-tailed possum on the road ahead of me, its red eyes shining at me in the headlights. Clarence Motz used to say "When the road gets too long and the night too dark, you're out of politics." Here I go, I said to myself. I turned around in a driveway and headed back home.

But, of course, the campaign went on, and by the next day, I was back on the trail again.

Six **Winning**

As everyone in Akron knows, the courthouse in Akron is on top of a hill and the steps are so steep no one ever uses them. In fact, for some time now, the approach to the big double front doors has been terraced and landscaped out of existence. Years ago, the alcove inside the unused front doors was a nesting area for a woman minister who performed marriages and for William V. Wallace, the *Akron Beacon Journal*'s tall, courtly, white-haired reporter who covered the courthouse from a battered desk there. If anyone had opened the front door, Bill and the minister might have been sucked out as if from an airlock.

People came and went through the more accessible basement doors beneath the steps. That made the lunch counter across from the elevators in the basement of the courthouse the traffic center of Akron. Everyone went by the counter some time and, with only one elevator in working order most of the time, passage was slow. I seldom went to the courthouse without a stop at the lunch counter for a good ten-cent cup of coffee. It was a place to see everyone. It was also the place to pick up the latest news and the titillating rumors that coursed through the courthouse every day.

Whenever I could lure her away from her desk, I used to meet Mary Ann Plant at the lunch counter. Mary Ann ran the county treasurer's office with conspicuous competence, first for Charlie Frank and, after his death, for Clyde H. Weil, known as "Kiddo," who was named to succeed Frank as he was considered more electable than Mary Ann.

I used to brag about knowing Mary Ann. She looked like an executive when there weren't many women executives around and none with her style, dash, and humor. Among her talents was the ability to fill up a campaign event with faithful supporters from the courthouse, thus giving to the uninitiated in attendance the impression of an outpouring of support for the candidates. Mary Ann was for equal pay for equal work long before anyone ever heard of women's liberation. She knew there was particularly

Mary Ann Plant, Assistant County Treasurer.

shocking discrimination in the amount paid to women at the courthouse. Taxpayers got some great bargains. It wasn't that the officeholders were mean. They just considered it a sufficient kindness to give a job to a needy widow. Yet, largely thanks to Mary Ann, most of the employees who turned out for meetings were women. That meant candidates got friendly faces wherever they went. Not all of the candidates appreciated that, however. Some candidates scorned meetings where they saw "the same old faces." Those candidates usually didn't last long in politics. The people whose familiar faces they scorned not only cast their own ballots but also were asked how to vote by many relatives and friends, and these were relatives and friends who were actually going to show up at the voting booths on election day.

Mary Ann couldn't evaluate how her friends were doing in a campaign because she was sure they would win, no matter what. But there was one person who could tell me how I was doing when I was running for the legislature. That was the man who ran the lunch counter, Ray Potts, a former sheriff who had been, shall we say, "active" in the days of Prohibition. I don't know for a fact that Ray's avocation was handicapping the local political races, but that was what I heard, so when Ray drew me away from the counter in the fall of 1954 and told me in a low voice that I was "looking good," I was excited and encouraged. I didn't know what I was doing right, but I resolved to do more of it.

I needed that encouragement because it was about then that I was recovering from a numbing encounter with robot typewriters—three typewriters, set in a half-circle in a back office at the Odd Fellows Temple, that could type a form letter over and over. A friend, Fred Shepard, got me the opportunity to use them at night to type campaign letters to about four hundred or so precinct committeemen. The typewriters were certainly not computers, but they had some early kind of memory. All I had to do was fill in the name and address of a committeeman and hit a button. The form letter would type itself while I addressed the next one at the next typewriter. Then I hit the button again and addressed still another at the third typewriter. By then, the first letter would be done, and I could start over. I pictured myself picking up the rhythm and moving gracefully from one typewriter to the next. I even planned on working my signature into the routine. I never did. At the end of an evening, I would come away so frazzled I could hardly find my way home. It's a good thing I was never obliged to make a living on an assembly line. The machines would have eaten me alive. When I finally finished the last of those letters, I thought any committeeman who got one *owed* me a vote. Candidates today don't know how good they have it with word processors and printers.

I'm sure I voted early on election day in 1954. Clarence Motz had taught me to do that on election day a year earlier. When I told him about four o'clock that I was leaving the office early to go vote, he was horrified that I hadn't voted already, first thing in the morning. "You might be dead by now!" he said. It was by no means clear whether it was my vote or me he would have missed more if I were dead, but I got the message.

Voting early made for a long day when I was on the ballot. Finally, however, evening came and most of us candidates would go to WAKR's television studios on Copley Road to hear the returns. WAKR had about seventy theater seats at the back of the former Copley movie theater and a set resembling a newsroom down front with blackboards where the returns were chalked up. I went in very hopeful about winning, but only the first returns were identified by precinct. We couldn't tell where the later ones were coming from, so even good numbers were ambiguous. Doubts began to dig in.

Winning an election is not like winning the lottery. It may not be a surprise, but it often takes a long while before totals can be depended on to indicate the final results. By the time I could be sure I was winning that first election in 1954, I was humble enough to be grateful. I was also so happy I was probably insufferable. But none of us took any joy in seeing others lose. One who was losing that night was John Ballard, the future mayor of Akron, a Republican nominee for state representative. He lost by only a few votes. I knew John's wife and sister and liked John. But friendship could carry me only so far. When the *Akron Beacon Journal* described the disappointment of "young John Ballard" the next day, I thought, "Young? He must be at least thirty!" I was twenty-seven.

Somehow I had never thought about what came after the election. But Mr. Motz did. He had a good friend, Ray Miller, who was the Democratic county chairman of Cuyahoga County. One of Miller's members of the House, Jim McGettrick, was running for reelection as minority leader, and he needed my vote. I soon learned that A. G. Lancione of Belmont County was also a candidate for minority leader, and he had a record that far outshone Jim McGettrick's. But Lancione didn't have the votes of the Cuyahoga County delegation that made up more than 40 percent of the Democrats elected to the House. And soon he didn't have my vote either, or the votes of the other two Democrats elected from Summit County, Thomas L. Thomas and George R. Madden. Mr. Motz let Ray Miller know McGettrick could count on us.

The Democratic caucus to choose the minority leader was held in December at a hotel in Warren. We heard a good speech from A. G. Lancione and a few words from Jim McGettrick, a pale, heavy man in an ill-fitted suit who knew he had the winning votes and so saw no need to waste his strength on charm. Then the vote was taken by secret ballot. Each of us wrote our choice on a card passed out to us. To my surprise, Tommy Thomas insisted on showing me his ballot with McGettrick's name plainly written on it. Why would he do that, I wondered. I voted for McGettrick, too, but I certainly didn't offer to show Tom my ballot. Tom knew McGettrick better than I did. When McGettrick's vote total was one less than expected, his forces were marshalled to find out who had failed to honor a commitment. The handwriting was analyzed on every ballot. If Tom had failed the test, my testimony would have been critical. Committee assignments rode on the outcome.

Not surprisingly, all of us who voted "right" got our first-choice committees. On Fred Harter's advice, I asked for the Judiciary Committee. On my own, I also asked for Commerce and Transportation and Financial Institutions. The idea was partly to avoid the usual Health, Conservation, Welfare, and Education Committees assigned to the few women members, but I had also heard that an interesting battle was likely to shape up in the Commerce and Transportation Committee on a proposal by Akron's AC&Y Railroad to build a Riverlake Belt Conveyor to haul coal and iron ore between the Ohio River and Lake Erie. The proposal was backed by Goodyear, which would supply the miles of rubber belting, and, of course, I was for Goodyear. It was opposed with fervor—and anything else required—by the railroad lobby, headed by a man named Pop Shively. I heard a lot about Pop Shively. He was said to run a round-the-clock poker game at the Deshler-Hilton Hotel where any member of the legislature was welcome to play and, it was also said, was very, very likely to win.

The legislature wasn't venal as far as I knew, but the cardroom could be attractive to some members. At that time, the legislature met only every other year for about six months, and the sessions ran from Monday night to

Thursday noon, but the salary was commensurately low—only $3,600 a year during my first term and $5,000 a year during my second and third terms. The bigger part was paid in the first year when the members had to pay for their own hotel rooms and meals, but it was never generous. The only allowance for expenses was ten cents a mile for travel once a week to and from Columbus during the session.

Members were also reimbursed for hotel and meals when they served between sessions on one or more Legislative Service Commission committees studying in depth some aspect of legislative policy. The committees didn't meet often, but provision for reimbursement was enough to make service on these committees popular. I once got a letter from the Internal Revenue Service which saw on my income tax return all the expenses for hotel and meals during the legislative session but only the small reimbursement I received for attending LSC committee meetings. The IRS was sure I must have received reimbursement for all the expenses I was claiming. I responded by citing the Ohio Constitution to show we were limited to our salaries and mileage for legislative sessions, but that wasn't good enough for the IRS. What its auditor wanted was a written statement to this effect from an official of the legislature. Carl Guess, the clerk of the House, gave me the necessary letter, enjoying the fact he outranked the Ohio Constitution.

The two months between the election in 1954 and the start of the legislative session in 1955 were probably the longest two months of my life. The legislature was due to convene on the first Monday in January 1955. Taking no chance on being late, I set out on Sunday. The family saw me off from the front porch, waving until I was out of sight. Although my 1951 De Soto burned about as much oil as gasoline, I was ready for every contingency. The car was stocked with water, a blanket, boots, a shovel, salt, homemade cookies, a first aid kit, and even a roll of toilet paper in a crocheted cover supplied by my aunt.

Does anyone else still remember the trip to Columbus before Interstate 71 opened? Back then the 125-mile trip was on two-lane roads bordered by deep ditches and took three and a half to four hours on Route 5 by way of Johnson's Corners in Barberton, Doylestown, Smithville, and a treacherous gully on the outskirts of Wooster, then Route 3 from Wooster through Loudonville (Harriet's Restaurant), over a roller coaster with banked turns, past a stand selling trail bologna at the top of a hill, and on to Mount Vernon (the Alcove Restaurant), Centerburg, Gahanna, and Columbus.

Clyde Mann, the reporter covering the legislature for the *Akron Beacon Journal,* had given me full instructions for staying at the Deshler-Hilton Hotel across from the statehouse. One dollar for the doorman, coming and going, to cover parking my car, and one dollar for Wilbur, the bellman, coming and going, to handle my bags. I added two dollars a week for the maid who stored some cushions and plants for me over the weekends. I think I remember the rooms ran about nine dollars a night. For less than thirty-five dollars a week during the sessions, I had perfect felicity for three terms.

Clyde didn't mention how to get to the House of Representatives. Of course, I knew it was in the statehouse, but where? It would have been terrible to ask. On the first day, I went into the statehouse and up a flight of stairs to the great hall under the rotunda, lined with glass cases holding the furled flags of Civil War regiments. I pretended to study the flags as I slowly turned around. At the top of one long double flight of marble stairs was a sign saying "House of Representatives." I walked up the stairs to a new world.

From the first day, I felt at home in the legislature—home in Cleveland, that is. When I located my assigned seat, I found Clevelanders to the right, Clevelanders to the left, and Clevelanders two deep behind me. The only reason I wasn't completely surrounded is that my seat was in the first row. Possibly the Cleveland delegation felt that an impressionable freshman would provide an extra vote when needed, although I was never actually solicited for a vote, even on a few occasions when the word was urgently passed all around me that LBS—Louis B. Seltzer, editor of the *Cleveland Press*—favored or disfavored some legislation.

Jim McGettrick, the surly Democratic minority leader, was a little hard to take, but otherwise I liked my Cuyahoga County neighbors, and the novelty of their ethnic mix intrigued me, coming as I did from Summit County where almost all the county and Akron officeholders had names of German or English origin. In the Cuyahoga delegation, Irish names were pre-

The floor of the Ohio House of Representatives, circa 1954.

dominant but were leavened with names like Novak, Horvath, Fuerst, and Sawicki. A dynastic bias was also evident—the only Republican member of the delegation, seated on the other side of the House, was Leonard Bartunek who undoubtedly owed his election to the popularity of Joe Bartunek, a Democratic senator. Calabrese was a Mafia family name in Cleveland, and Tony Calabrese was said to have come from Cleveland's notorious Short Vincent Street, but he undoubtedly got his votes from having a name like "Celebrezze," not from the Mafiosi. Anthony Celebrezze was a popular mayor of Cleveland, later secretary of Health, Education and Welfare under Presidents Kennedy and Johnson, and then a judge of the U.S. Sixth Circuit Court of Appeals in Cincinnati. We not only had a Sweeney, a Sullivan, and a Corrigan, good old Cleveland ballot names, but we had two Gormans—one in the House and one in the Senate, and later another one in the House. My favorite was James P. "Seamus" Kilbane, who modestly acknowledged a relationship to a former member named Johnny Kilbane, a famous Cleveland boxer in the olden days. (I thought of claiming Terry McGovern, another famous boxer, but decided against it.)

What kept puzzling me was that some Clevelanders I met had what sounded to me like a Brooklyn accent. The mystery was solved when a former Cleveland member who had come to visit spoke with an unmistakable Irish brogue, and I recognized it was related to that "Brooklyn" accent. I recognized something more. The brogue brought back memories of my Grandfather McGovern from Clearfield, Pennsylvania, who died when I was seven. But when I reported this to my father, he got very hot about it. "Your grandfather did not have a brogue," he said. "He was an educated man!" It was true my grandfather was educated. As a young man, he had taken the only route to education open to a poor Irishman in Ulster (County Cavan) by studying for the priesthood. He was said to have spoken Latin and French fluently. But I was sure it was his Irish voice I had heard again.

There were a few other "native wood-notes wild": a nasal twang from Cincinnati and, from southeastern Ohio, a few members who sat on "chers" and "weeshed" for the best. I myself might have been noted by others as saying "warsh rag," but luckily the subject of washcloths never came up. There were also some cultural overtones. One day when the electronic switchboard that recorded members' votes went haywire, the gentleman from Lawrence, Mr. Siple, rose to report to the Speaker that the "tote board" had the wrong total. Perhaps it should not be mentioned that one member (who was absolutely *not* typical) was famously reported to have said, "They ain't going to buy me for no sangwich."

One reason I liked that front row-seat was that it often put me face to face with Clyde Mann, the reporter for the *Akron Beacon Journal*—"Paisan" to many of his friends because of his sunny Italian disposition and stocky build. When the House was in session, the newspapermen covering the General Assembly sat at desks attached to the fronts of the front-row desks. I enjoyed Clyde's comments on machinations and members. They were on target and often funny. But Clyde never suggested how to vote. If he disagreed with me, I knew it only because he would ask me to give him a statement to go in his story. Sometimes several of us rode to Columbus in Clyde's car. Clyde would slow down at a high point just south of Loudonville, a signal for us to open the windows, flap the doors, and yell at the top of our lungs. I never knew why we did this or how it got started, but that was half of what made it fun. The other half was probably that we simply liked being crazy together. It tells a lot about Clyde that his license number was 1 YQ 2.

Next to Clyde usually sat Howard Thompson, called "Sam," from the *Ohio State Journal.* Sam and I both took a simple and excessive pleasure in puns. He was glad to have someone new to tell about the escape clause in the pardon and parole bill and the grandfather clause in the aid for the aged bill. Every session had a proposal for a tax on soft drinks, and Sam would say with great relish, "You can tax my daddy, but you can't tax my pop." I told Sam about an imaginary greenhouse bill so I could report that my cosponsors had taken French leaves. Sam said he had heard some cutting remarks, but he was rooting for the bill.

The kidding is mutual between Clyde Mann (kibitzing) and Summit County Reps. Frances McGovern, Elizabeth Smith, Charles Madden in Ohio House of Representatives.

Kidding around with Elizabeth Smith, Clyde Mann, and Charles Madden in the Ohio House of Representatives, 1959.

The newspapermen also had working desks in a newsroom off a passage around the rotunda. The passage, which lay between the House and the Senate, was very narrow, but it was much used because it was the only way to get from one house to the other that didn't require a long trip down one side of the statehouse, across, and up the other side. I have heard the newsroom was moved long ago to permit the passage to be widened. That's progress for you: two steps forward, one step back. There were days when the only evidence of cooperation between the two houses of the legislature was the members' avoidance of bone-jarring encounters with each other in the old "Narrows."

The women of the legislature were a special group—five of us in the House and one in the Senate in my first term. There was some beauty in small numbers. We had our own sitting room at the back of the House chamber and a matron of the majority party whose only duty was to visit with us. As individuals, we couldn't have been more different, but we got along well. Ethel Swanbeck from Erie County was a doctor's wife, a white-haired matron who had been a mathematics teacher. We had breakfast to-

gether every morning at the hotel, and I was very fond of her. Clara Weisenborn was the food and garden editor of the *Dayton Journal Herald.* She was
the most good-humored, except as regards food. She was our taster when we
ate together ("I suppose they *call* this Hollandaise . . .") and she often sent
food back. Loretta Cooper Woods, a librarian from Scioto County, was
blond, blue-eyed, sweet, obliging, and very, very Republican—the total an-
tithesis of Vernal Riffe, who succeeded her when the Democrats got the majority in my third term. In time, Vern became the hard-nosed Speaker of the
House. We liked Golda Mae Edmonston, an active club woman, but didn't
see much of her because she was from Columbus and had a home, not a hotel, to return to when sessions were over. Over in the Senate was Bess Gorman, an old-timer from Cleveland. She gave her occupation as "parliamen-
tarian," but as far as I could see she was first of all a good politician. We
shared a delight we kept secret from the other "girls." When, as often happened, a lobbyist chose to entertain the women as a group, drinks would be
offered all around. Bess would order bourbon on the rocks or some such,
and I usually had a martini. Clara, however, would say, "Oh, I think I'll just
have a Pink Lady," and the others, with a self-deprecating nod to the waiter,
would say they'd "just" have the same. Bess would give me a huge wink, and
we shared secret smiles. There is nothing "just" about a Pink Lady except its
dainty name.

One day the women members were invited to lunch by three or four elderly suffragettes. We met at the Maramor, our favorite restaurant near the
statehouse, but the meeting was awkward. It was an occasion for us to express our appreciation for what they had made possible, and probably we
did say thank you in a perfunctory way. But all I remember is that they
beamed proudly at us. Their emotion embarrassed me, and, cruelly, I was
embarrassed for them, that they should be so thrilled by our unimportant
victories. But I have remembered that luncheon, while almost all others
have been forgotten. There are very few moments in my life that I would like
to relive, but that is one of them. It wasn't until years later that I realized

what the suffragettes had done for us and understood why our elections, which we took for granted, were like personal victories to them.

The composition of our group of women changed in my third term. Loretta Cooper Woods and Golda Mae Edmonston were swept away in a Democratic tide in 1958. Only Ethel Swanbeck and Clara Weisenborn survived, but we gained in number. Anne Donnelly was elected from Cleveland, Bernice MacKenzie from Canton, and Betty Smith joined me from Summit County, succeeding her husband after he died unexpectedly in 1958. As before, we were all good friends without regard to party, although we now had a Democratic matron in our ladies lounge, patronage being matronage as regards that position. I eventually lost touch with Anne and Betty when I was no longer in the legislature, but Bernice MacKenzie, later Bernice Frease, was one of my closest friends until she died in 1990. We lived only twenty miles away from each other, but, since neither of us had the telephone habit, we mostly kept in touch with long, newsy letters. Bernice was also a lawyer, and, what with both of us being politicians and Democrats, we thought we had the same interests until we took a trip to England together and found we had different views on whether to go to museums or go shopping.

RE-ELECT

FRANCES McGOVERN

DEMOCRAT

STATE REPRESENTATIVE

Practicing Attorney · Seven Years
Graduate Akron University — Western Reserve University
Active in Civic Affairs
Now Serving You in the Legislature

Thanks —
Fran McGovern

Hand card from 1956 election.

Women of the Ohio House of Representatives, 1959. *L to R:* **Bernice MacKenzie, Ethel Swanbeck, me, Anne Donnelly, Clara Weisenborn, and Betty Smith.**

I was a little surprised to find I particularly liked the members from the rural counties, who made up the Cornstalk Brigade. Most of them were farmers or lawyers or insurance men from small towns. One listed himself as a "grain elevator," which required some of us to reflect a while. But these were no bumpkins. They were smart, they were wise, and one in particular had a great sense of humor. That was Virgil Perrill from Fayette County, the hero of the Battle of the Statehouse Garage.

Those who park in the garage under the statehouse today may have difficulty believing it wasn't always there. But it almost wasn't built. The bill to create it was hard fought by both sides in the House Judiciary Committee, and we who were members of the committee were flown to Chicago to see a successful underground facility. Opponents insisted we also see an automated aboveground garage a couple of blocks away. That garage had elevators that lifted cars into slots. They were open-sided and traveled by the most direct route to the nearest opening. A gang of about twenty of us on one elevator ended up clutching each other in panic when the elevator took us up on a diagonal path.

Virgil Perrill attacked the underground parking garage bill with a counterproposal. It failed to turn the tide but became an instant "best seller" in the Bill Room, where copies of bills were handed out. Perrill's bill purported to direct the construction of the garage, making elaborate and extended provisions, with tongue in cheek, for moving all the statues on the statehouse lawn. Special concern was indicated for the one known as "The Mother of the Gracchi and Her Sons, the Jewels of Ohio," the sons being Ohio presidents and Salmon P. Chase. Most appreciated, however, was the bill's provision creating a special commission to locate a new site for Ohio's Capitol, "keeping in mind its future usefulness as a parking facility."

The Mother of the Gracchi was probably seriously displeased when she and her boys were moved into storage and construction began. No doubt the squirrels were also displeased when their trees disappeared and the people who fed them were fenced away. But I for one was relieved that the promises not to change the statehouse itself were being kept. One of my favorite features seemed most vulnerable—the walls of old stables between the statehouse and its annex, reached at ground level on each side through little doors set in full-sized garage doors. One ducked one's head and stepped up and over the sills of those little doors like Alice in Wonderland after she ate that famous piece of cake and grew too big for a time. The governor and a couple of other favored officials parked their cars in the stables. I believe I got a greater sense of history from the stables than I did from the glass cases upstairs filled with the Civil War battle flags. The stables, once occupied by horses and splendid carriages, were a bridge to the past that never failed to move me, notwithstanding the anomaly of cars within them and, later, cars below them in the new garage.

I didn't appreciate as much the members' historic desks, although the opportunity to lift and drop the hinged lids—oh, so gently—did offer a means of expression to members bored or put off by some speeches. Since the desks were arrayed in half circles in front of the Speaker's marble throne, there were small wedges of space between them for stuffing bills and other papers in there, one by one. By the time the legislature was ready to adjourn, stick dynamite would have been the best, if not the most acceptable, way to free up the accumulations. Most were hopelessly left behind. One of the nicest perquisites of being chairman of the House Judiciary Committee in my third term was an office of my own, but that only permitted me to accumulate more paper. By adjournment, the office looked like a warehouse in a windstorm.

Eight "Miss Representative"

Courtesy titles were the order of the day in the legislature. It amused people to call me "Miss Representative," but officially I was "the lady from Summit, Miss McGovern." The official titles were used over and over in the early days of my first term because at that time it was the custom of the House to accept the introduction of bills, one by one, from the floor during the sessions, recognizing the sponsor each time by his or her name and title. A member wishing to introduce a bill would rise and be recognized by the Speaker as, for example, "the gentleman from Wayne, Mr. Fisher." The member would then hand his bill to a page who would take it to Carl Guess, the clerk of the House, stationed in front of the Speaker's throne. The clerk or an assistant in good voice would read the bill number, sponsor's name, and the title of the bill—officially, the "first reading" of the bill. All of this used up a preposterous amount of time. Later it was changed so that bills were filed in the clerk's office and the clerk just read off the titles seriatim at the beginning of the sessions. Time-consuming as the old practice was, I am glad it prevailed when I was a new member, because it helped us get to know each other. While the members were recognized the same way for every other purpose, it was the repetition with the introduction of bills that had special value to me. To this day, I can read off the names of a great many members and their counties in my head and even see them before me, standing up with bills in hand.

That practice had another value that first year. We had a page with red hair and a stocky build who excited admiring murmurs from the balconies when he sped up and down the aisles to pick up the members' bills. We soon realized the audience was in the balconies to see him, not us. He seemed unconscious of the attention he was getting, but his name was "Hopalong" Cassady, and everyone in the balconies knew it. Columbus, we outlanders learned, was a football town. Ohio State University was valued chiefly for its football team, and Hopalong Cassady was the star of that team. He outshone

Roger Cloud, the Speaker of the House, and all the members. Any member carried away by the glory of election was quickly reduced to size when measured against the real values of the playing field.

Other pages drew little attention, even from the members. They might as well have been wallpaper. But the walls had ears. I had a friend who was a page in the Senate, Jim Davis from home, a law student at Ohio State who had been appointed a page by Fred Harter. From time to time, I used to drink beer with Jim and some other pages at the Ringside, a little pub in an alley across from the statehouse. I learned far more about what was going on in the legislature from Jim and his friends than I ever could have learned on my own. Jim, who practices law in Akron, is still a friend, one of my best friends to this day.

The first bills I handed to a page were a dull lot—six minor bills given to me by the Department of Highway Safety—but one of them got me off to a good start. It moved easily through committee and soon turned up "above the black line" on the legislative calendar, meaning it would soon be scheduled for a vote on the House floor. A lot of agony went into composing my first, very brief, speech, but I had already learned that a "corrective" bill, being uncontroversial, was sure to pass. Bills that "did only one thing" usually passed easily, too. (One member said he was going to get up some day with a proposal and say, "This bill is purely corrective. It does only one thing. It wipes out the state of Ohio." He expected it would pass unanimously.) My bill fit the formula. "This bill is corrective," I said. "It does only one thing." Only a few more words were needed to say what was being corrected. I got some smiles and even a little applause. The members were pleased I was learning the game.

One might suppose representatives came to the legislature to act upon a political philosophy, but I don't think that was common. I, for one, didn't begin with a political philosophy, and I never did acquire one, at least not consciously. While I thought it would be nice to be of service, and I also thought I would enjoy the public eye, one reason I ran for the legislature was for the money. I was reasonably sure I could win, and in my financial circumstances, the salary, trifling though it was, looked very good to me. The main reason I ran, however, was that I thought it would be interesting. In the beginning, I didn't even have any causes, although I acquired quite a few. Beyond that, I thought it was sufficient to be honest and to know right from wrong.

It was never that simple. Honesty about money or favors was never a problem, but intellectual honesty was a little trickier. If I wanted to vote a certain way, it was always easy to find a "good" reason to do so. Rightness or wrongness was also not a dependable guide. I discovered that early on when a bill was proposed by the trucking industry that called for shortening the hitch on semis for safety reasons. The state Highway Department denied that the longer hitch had any effect on safety and said that the shorter hitch would increase damage to roadways. Which was right? Which was wrong? I didn't know then, and evidently I still don't, because I can't remember how I voted.

I found, as most do, that I pretty much called each bill on its own terms. Even "moral" issues I decided for reasons neither moral nor immoral. One bill was intended to restore movie censorship in some form after it had been found unconstitutional. My vote against the bill proceeded from observing the censors almost licking their lips when they showed us self-righteously what they had cut from films.

In 1959, capital punishment was the issue. Our committee hearing the bill visited the death house at the old penitentiary on Long Street, a few blocks from the statehouse. It was a small brick building with a cell for the condemned prisoner next to an old-fashioned oaken chair that, but for the shackles, was not unlike the mission-style chairs in my great-aunt's living room. My vote was against capital punishment after I looked at the dull, al-most witless eyes in many of the photographs on the wall of those who had been executed. I couldn't help wondering if all of them were guilty. The per-sistent smell of burnt flesh probably influenced me even more. I had to be taken to the door at one point to get some fresh air.

Of course, on partisan issues I was a Democrat, but there weren't many such issues. Unless contrived, there are no obvious party positions on most subjects of state legislation. Labor issues were the exception—always partisan. Even on these, I sometimes needed a little coaching. I remember the stricken silence that greeted my answer when I was asked by the AFL-CIO Council during my first campaign whether I believed in the right to work. It sounded good to me, and I said so. The "right to work," I was then told plainly, was a euphemism for legislation to ban the union shop; this was anathema to labor and thus to Democrats. As it happened, though, Democrats had reason to be grateful for the issue. Despite their opposition, a proposed right-to-work law was put on the ballot in 1958. Labor exhorted union members and their families to "Vote No on Issue 2," and a major effort was made to ensure a big turnout. The voters who turned out not only defeated the right-to-work proposal, but they also voted for every Democrat in sight. That gave the Democrats the governor, Michael V. DiSalle, and the majority in the legislature in 1959. It also gave me the unexpected opportunity to be chairman of the House Judiciary Committee. After a big discussion in the committee, it was decided that I was to be "Madam Chairman," although neither man nor madam. There was no such word as "chairperson" in those days, and we would have laughed if we had heard it.

Another exception as a partisan issue was the proposal to create a Fair Employment Practices Commission, the only proposal I can remember in my three terms in the legislature that touched on civil rights, even tangentially. The difference between the parties was not so much over whether such a commission should be created, although there was a lot more enthusiasm for it on the Democratic side of the House than on the Republican side. Given that a bill was likely to be enacted in 1959, when the Democrats had the majority, the big difference was over whether the commission's rules should require compliance or whether they should be merely educational. Recalling the history of other statutory reforms, such as child labor laws, I believed the best way to educate was to put new practices into effect so that, after a time, old practices would become unthinkable.

I was lucky in encountering many issues at their turning points during my period in the legislature. The treatment of the mentally ill is a case in point. I was already interested in the subject, after having been on a local United Community Council committee on mental health, chaired by Judge Stephen C. Colopy. At that time, in the early 1950s, Summit County had two mental hospitals—Hawthornden State Hospital and Cuyahoga Falls Receiving Hospital—but only one psychiatrist, Benjamin Moorstein, no outpatient care except for children, and no treatment available in general hospitals. The Summit County Mental Health Association and the Mental Hygiene Clinic both grew out of the committee's interest, and I was an incorporator of the Mental Health Association and, in time, served on both boards. The usual approach to mental illness, however, continued for many years to be walling up the patients in state mental hospitals.

The tide turned in 1955. It began with the shocking news that mentally ill patients at Apple Creek State Hospital in Wayne County were being treated with drugs, and five or six had died. There was no reason to conclude that drug treatment was the cause of death, but that was the popular conclusion. Our delegation, except for me, introduced a resolution condemning the hospital's treatment. Dr. Robert Haines, superintendent of Apple Creek and later director of the state Department of Mental Hygiene and Correction, was brought before a legislative committee to respond. For the first time, we began to hear what drugs could do to control effects of mental illness. Dr. Porterfield, director of the department, also asked that a $150-million bond issue be put on the ballot to improve facilities in the neglected hospitals. That was a huge sum at the time, but the issue passed in 1955. Meanwhile, Ray Miller Jr. of Cleveland and I got an appropriation of $1.7 million to build a 100-bed children's mental hospital at Hawthornden State Hospital, in Sagamore Hills midway between Akron and Cleveland. What would that build today? The authorization was a reaction to news of a fourteen-year-old boy being incarcerated with adults in Cleveland State Hospital. Roger Sherman, of Children's Hospital in Akron, and Lou Kacalieff, of the Akron Child Guidance Center, were the principal proponents. I am the one who got garbage dumped on my front lawn, however, presumably from neighbors of the hospital in Sagamore Hills who didn't welcome it one bit.

The children's hospital was never fully occupied. Medical treatment and local outpatient services for mental illness advanced so fast that institutional treatment for children—and indeed for adults too—became less and less important. As with many of my interests from legislative days, I stayed involved in mental health issues for many years. I helped create the Portage Path Community Mental Health Center, served on the advisory board for the Sagamore Hills hospital, and was on the first "648 board," a precursor of today's Alcohol, Drug Addiction, and Mental Health Services (ADM) Board. Successful community treatment of mental illness, which was almost unthinkable in 1955, is today the rule. The hopeless lockups of the past are gone. I like remembering I was there at the beginning.

Nine The Past as Prologue

Not all my recurring memories from legislative days are literally legislative. Members were assumed to have influence, and many were the calls I got to "use my influence" to solve some problem. My mother used to think constituents were clairvoyant, able to see me driving in the driveway at home on Thursdays when the weekly sessions ended, able even to see when she was about to put dinner on the table, because it was then the telephone would start to ring for me. Whenever I go through the intersection of Smith Road and Ghent Road (Route 176), which is often, I am reminded of a request in 1955 to "use my influence" to get a traffic light installed there, because views of the crossing at the top of a low hill were impeded by dips and slopes in three directions.

Dutifully, I relayed the request for a light to the state Highway Department. Someone who sounded thoroughly exasperated said there was very little traffic at that intersection and a record of only minor fender-benders. My influence was only good enough to get a blinker light installed. But that was before Summit Mall was built at that intersection and long before the developments at Montrose, once the quiet scene of little more than a drive-in theater and a miniature golf course and swim club. When the traffic picked up for all the new destinations, a stoplight was installed without anyone having to ask for it. By 1999, the whole intersection had to be reconfigured with five lanes and long, nearly level approaches. I'm probably the only one who still sees the old scene when I drive through.

My memory goes back not one step but two when I see Key Bank branches—first to Key Bank's predecessor, Society Bank, and then to the Society for Savings in a big, dark Richardson Romanesque stone building on the north side of Cleveland Public Square. I recall the battle of the titans, Cleveland Trust Company vs. The Society for Savings, in our little backwater Financial Institutions Committee in 1955. Branch banking was still new in the 1950s. Cleveland Trust and other banks were authorized to establish branch banks by the Ohio Superintendent of Banks, but the Society for Savings couldn't open any branches because it wasn't a bank. It was a mutual savings association created by a special act of the legislature more than one hundred years earlier. There was only one other like it, the Society for Savings in Springfield, Ohio.

The battle began with a bill to permit the Society to establish branches. The big wheels of Cleveland Trust immediately began to turn. The Society was new to the legislative world and incredibly naive. Cleveland Trust was not. The bill was turned inside out. It not only did not permit Society branches, it specifically prohibited them! I voted with the Society, to no avail, but Senator Fred Harter saved the day when the bill got to the Senate. He turned the bill inside out again, this time to permit the Society to reorganize as a bank after making special provision to protect balances in the old savings accounts of lost heirs. As a bank, it would then be eligible to open branches like other banks. When the bill came back to the House for concurrence in the Senate amendments, its sponsor, Frank Gorman of Cleveland, once in despair, said smoothly that the amendments were "corrective," and they passed. Against the odds, the Society for Savings had won. It soon became Society Bank and began opening branches.

Just how naive the Society was at that time, however, was proved after the legislature adjourned. There was certainly nothing the matter with the very nice thank-you letter I got from Jim Weeks, attorney for the Society, that I have saved and still treasure. But, perhaps thinking they were acting like the pros, "friends" at the Society also sent me a package in the mail. When I opened it, it contained a diamond wristwatch! I quickly mailed it back. Fred Harter said he got a sterling silver tea set and mailed it back just as quickly. We "settled" instead for a Cleveland Indians baseball game in a grand box at the old stadium. Several years later, when Fred's son was getting married, a wedding present arrived for the son. It was the tea set. Fred said he gave up at that point, and told his son to keep it.

Sometimes it is failure rather than success that jogs my memory. How to finance schools is an ongoing concern that recalls for me the early efforts to equalize the local burden of school support through the formula for distributing state money under the School Foundation program. There was and is a great disparity in the tax duplicates of the various school districts. Every new formula we tried that would equalize support in some places would make matters worse somewhere else, so we gave up. We knew that pooling part of the proceeds of local millage for redistribution on a needs basis would help equalize support, but the school districts losing money to the pool would have slaughtered anyone with the temerity to vote for that remedy. The idea has come up again and again since then, more recently as a possible means of dealing with the Ohio Supreme Court's ruling that the present method of state funding of public schools is unconstitutional. How enactment of that idea would have pleased a representative from Toledo in my day, a Mr. Reynolds, who had run for the legislature solely to effect equalization. Like most "single-issue" types, his eyes lit up with manic zeal on the subject. He lashed out at all of us for failing, and he quit the legislature after one term. I have no sympathy for the failure to provide adequate state support for schools, but even now, more than forty years later, I read with real sympathy of new efforts to equalize the local tax burdens.

One memory turned up recently like a bad penny—the memory of a failure to do what we knew we should do when we were reforming the minor courts in 1957. One of the reforms was to end the notorious invitations from some mayors to the State Highway Patrol to drag in speeders from all over to the local mayors' courts so as to increase local revenue from fines. But we didn't want to stir up the mayors any more than absolutely necessary. All we did was confine the jurisdiction of mayors' courts to municipal boundaries, although we knew perfectly well there was the same conflict of interest within those boundaries. More than forty years later, in 1999, a federal court threw out a conviction by the mayor's court of Macedonia because of the mayor's interest in the revenue produced by the fine. Now perhaps the legislature will do what we failed to do: do away with mayor's courts altogether.

The boldest of our reforms to the minor courts did away with justices of the peace in Ohio. Another created a new system of minor county courts to take the place of the justices in areas outside the jurisdiction of municipal courts. These changes were being led by Kenneth Robinson of Marion County. My only contribution was to extend the territorial jurisdiction of Summit County's three municipal courts so that no minor courts were needed in Summit County, but I took a great deal of interest in all the reforms.

It was at that time that a friend from Akron, Hobart Schaefer, a rubber worker from Goodrich, used to ride back and forth to Columbus with me fairly often. He was a big man with the tonsure of a monk and the dignity of a bishop. I loved having him ride along because he had an original but wonderful gift with words. For example, he didn't trust what he called his old "jalopidated" car, although, he said, it "clumb an eminence" as well as any car on the road. What was bringing him to the legislature was principally workmen's compensation legislation ("workers' compensation" today.) But I told him about the court reforms we were working on, and he said he had a natural interest in them, because his grandfather had been a justice of the peace. In fact, he said, he still had his grandfather's law book. I told him about the time I walked nearly a quarter of a mile down a railroad track to file a case with a railroad worker who was a justice of the peace. The man walked me back to his car to record the filing. On the seat was *Swann's Treatise,* the bible of the justices of the peace. "That's the book!" my friend said. He told me he now was a great supporter of municipal courts because of an experience he had in the Cincinnati Municipal Court when a retarded member of his family was picked up for vagrancy or something of the sort. "I pleaded mercy, and the judge coincided," he said. I never could have thought of a way to say that so succinctly and so well. I added his testimonial, suitably rephrased, to the support of the Akron Bar Association for extending the jurisdiction of the local municipal courts.

One reminder from the past came as a big surprise but also a great satisfaction to me. In 1957 and 1959, I cosponsored with Fritz Cassel of Wyandot

County a bill to do away with sales tax stamps. Roger Cloud joined in sponsoring the bill in 1959. The stamps were originally intended to get merchants to prepay sales tax during the Depression. The system devised to achieve that purpose wasn't very successful, but it did give many people an interest in perpetuating it. The state treasurer had the privilege of choosing the agents who sold the stamps to merchants. The agents got 1 percent of the proceeds as their commission. Merchants were to give the stamps as receipts to customers for paying the tax, but they could delay buying them because customers didn't always ask for the stamps. Customers were encouraged to ask for their stamps because they could give them to charities. Charities could then redeem the stamps for three cents on the dollar. Merchants could also give big blocks of late-purchased stamps to charity. As might be expected, the treasurer, agents, merchants, charities, and many customers did not take kindly to proposals to do away with the stamps. The biggest charitable beneficiary was a veterans' post. The next largest was a little church in the boondocks favored by car dealers whose customers seldom thought to ask for stamps when they bought their cars. Many other charities were affected by the bill. To say the least, doing away with the stamps was controversial.

Our stamp bill failed when the legislative majority was of the same party as the state treasurer, first Republican in 1957 and then Democratic in 1959. That was an interesting enough reason to remember it. (It finally passed in 1961 when the treasurer was a Democrat but the legislative majority was Republican.) What made it especially memorable to me, however, was a certain lobbyist, a tall, spare man with rimless glasses and a bearing of dry rectitude who purported to represent the Catholic bishop of Cincinnati in exhorting me to give up my pursuit of this legislation. If I persisted, he told me, he would see to it that I never got another Catholic vote. This was the rawest pitch I had made to me in the entire time I served in the legislature, so I remembered his name when I forgot many others. Some years later, his name came up in national news about savings and loan scandals. It was Charles Keating Jr.

One of the things I am proudest of is helping to repair the county charter amendment to the Ohio Constitution, Article X, Section 3. This is the section Summit County has used to alter the form of its county government and to create a council that can enact ordinances to meet local needs. The county charter amendment, adopted in 1933, was made useless in 1936 by the Ohio Supreme Court in *Howland v. Krause*, 130 Ohio St. 455. In that case, the court held that a charter giving a county any powers *like* those exercised by municipalities would require adoption by the four majorities required for adoption of a county charter taking powers *away from* municipalities. The four majorities were required in the largest city, outside the largest city, in the county, and in each of a majority of townships, villages, and cities in the county. Someone speculated that in Cuyahoga County, with its multiple subdivisions, a charter could be defeated even with 90 percent of the voters voting in its favor.

I happened on this barrier to adoption of county charters while exploring another kind of home rule charter that would permit a federation of local units of government to perform duties assigned by a charter. The result was that I joined Kenneth Berry of Coshocton County and Jack Chester of Franklin County in proposing to restore the county charter amendment to its original intent, and they joined me in proposing authority to adopt "metropolitan federation" charters. The county charter issue, which we also amended to reduce the four majorities required for major change to three in counties with populations over 500,000, passed on the 1957 state ballot. Alas, the metropolitan federation amendment landed on the same ballot with the right-to-work issue in 1958 and was defeated by all those "no" votes. The legislature voted to submit the federation issue again in 1959, but it was kept off the ballot by a technicality: the failure of the Senate clerk to print the proposal in the Senate journal. Later, Ed Garrigan, elected to represent Summit County in the Ohio Senate in 1962, proposed the issue again under the name of United Service Authority (USA for short), but it failed, and no one has tried since to resurrect it.

Significantly, Summit County was one of the few counties that voted "yes" on metropolitan federations even while voting "no" on the right-to-work proposal. This openness in Summit County to reshaping government to meet local needs encouraged tries for county charters in 1970 and 1973. (I was elected to the commission that proposed the 1970 charter.) Both attempts were too ambitious, and they failed. But then the Goals for Greater Akron group proposed a further amendment to the Ohio Constitution to permit a county charter to be submitted directly to voters, without election of a charter commission and a year's wait on its proposal. This passed, and soon after, so did the prudently modest initial proposals for change in our unique county charter, directly submitted in 1979 and effective in 1980.

Without current reminders, it's not easy to remember other bills, but in the period I served, from 1955 to 1960, I got a fair number of bills passed. They included a procedure for adopting a state building code tied to performance rather than specifications, licensing of practical nurses, the Uniform Commercial Code, three bills sponsored with the Bob Taft of my day to liberalize opportunities for epileptics, the point system for traffic offenses, outlawing of a debt-pooling racket, payroll checkoffs by state employees for United Way, equal pay for equal work, regulation of charitable solicitations, and creation of the first Department of Industrial and Economic Development for Ohio, known unfortunately as "DIED," which foreshadowed its fate. It was succeeded by the Department of Development of Ohio, called "DODO," which some would say foreshadowed its performance.

One bill I had very little to do with ended up with my name on it as a cosponsor, and I didn't complain. Introduced by Andy Devine of Toledo to define ambulances as emergency vehicles, it was amended by the gallant Judiciary Committee in 1957 to add my name and the name of Joe Lady of Hardin County to the title. It passed as the "Devine, Lady, Miss McGovern" bill.

Some legislation I sponsored that was intended to make a difference at home had no impact here. One was a bill permitting tuition-free enrollment for some students outside the municipalities served by Ohio's three municipal universities in Akron, Toledo, and Cincinnati. It was superseded upon their becoming state universities. A bill to facilitate the combination of health districts has been used elsewhere but not in Summit County, which still has three separate districts.

Therein lies a tale. The combined health board bill was uncontroversial and easy to get passed after I voted "right" a couple of times to persuade Roy H. Longenecker, the chairman of the House Health Committee, to set it down for hearing. All it did was permit an agreement of combination to set out the size and composition of the combined board, which would otherwise be narrowly limited. It was a controversial bill for me to sponsor, however, because back when I was practicing law in Barberton, I used to lunch every day at the Elks Club with a group that included Kate Wallace, the secretary of the Barberton Health Department. The lunch group was horrified when I proposed what could mean the end of Kate's job, although only if a merger were agreed upon and then only if she was thrown to the wolves. And that wasn't all! My landlord on Fourth Street in Barberton had been Dr. Finefrock, the Barberton director of health. Dr. Finefrock was a grand old man, much revered in Barberton. I used to say hello and how are you when I'd see him coming into his office on the first floor. He always said "Better." One day I asked him if he had been ill. "Oh, no," he said. "I don't say I'm fine because then whoever I'm talking to will start telling me, 'Well, Doc, I haven't been so well' and go on and on. If I say 'better,' that ends it. No one wants to hear my troubles, so they spare me theirs." Plainly, Dr. Finefrock was canny enough to protect his own bailiwick. To me, it has never made sense to have three health boards in Summit County, but there is something to be said for the reason we still have them: all the directors have been popular and good.

I think I did as much legislating by serving on subcommittees as I did by getting bills enacted. I liked playing around with the phrasing of bills that weren't clear and trying to resolve differences. My willingness—in fact eagerness—to work on many subcommittees in my first term was possibly one reason I was given a wonderful lift in my second term. I needed the lift, because when in 1957, I got a second chance to vote for the Democratic minority leader, I voted for A. G. Lancione of Bellaire instead of Jim McGettrick of Cleveland. McGettrick won anyway, and since he was a mean-spirited man, reprisal was swift. I was assigned to a couple of committees so obscure I can't remember what they were. I appealed to Roger Cloud, the Republican Speaker of the House, and lo, I was on Judiciary again, and on interesting new committees on Metropolitan Affairs and Elections and Federal Relations to which major policy bills were steered. And all this bounty came with no strings attached.

Happily, no one thought to change my seat, so I was still "at home" with the Cleveland delegation.

Ten From Rights-of-Way to Going Away

Pop Shively, the chief lobbyist for the railroads, was testifying before the House Commerce and Transportation Committee in 1955. "The AC&Y Railroad," he said. "That's supposed to be short for the Akron, Canton, and Youngstown Railroad. But the railroad doesn't go to Canton. It doesn't go to Youngstown. You know what I call it? I call it the 'A railroad.'" Pop Shively obviously did not count the "A Railroad" as one of his fold. The reason was that AC&Y's baby, the Riverlake Belt Conveyor, was intended to take business from railroads by hauling coal to Lake Erie from the Ohio River and bringing back iron ore.

The AC&Y hoped the legislature would give Riverlake the power of eminent domain to acquire rights-of-way. It could buy most of what it needed the same way it could acquire land for any other purpose, but its conveyor belt would cross over railroad tracks at several points, and no railroad would think of selling it the right-of-way unless forced to do so. I joined the fray with enthusiasm in the House committee. Here was an Akron project that brought Akronites to Columbus—notably Bart Stewart, Vincent Johnson, and Joe Savely from AC&Y, and Frank Quirk and others from Goodyear because the conveyor belt, many miles long, would be made by Goodyear.

As Clyde Mann reported in the *Akron Beacon Journal,* Shively testified in the committee hearings that the bill before us was unfair in proposing eminent domain without all the burdens of railroad regulation. I said I didn't understand what was unfair. "It's simple," Shively said. "If you and I were playing poker, we would play by the same rules." "But would I be dealt the same number of cards to begin the game?" I asked him. Shively had no answer, but he didn't need one. He was winning. The bill was losing. In a twenty-one-member committee, the vote was expected to be ten for, eleven against.

There was only one vote we could hope to change. Tom Gindlesberger of Holmes County was leaning to the railroad position but maybe wasn't absolutely committed yet. My uncle's wife was related to the probate judge of Holmes County. That gave Joe Savely and me the crazy idea of asking him to sound Tom Gindlesberger out.

The judge received us very cordially one Saturday afternoon. A young Amish girl in a white bonnet served us big tumblers of cider. I tasted the cider and found it shockingly sharp, unlike any cider I had ever had, but I sipped it politely while we explained our problem. The judge didn't know Tom well and doubted he could help us but wanted to know just what our bill was and what we needed. The discussion went on for some time. Meanwhile the little Amish girl was refilling my glass to the brim every time I managed a few sips. At length we stood up to go. I couldn't believe it! The room turned dark. My eyes wanted to cross. My knees bent in the wrong direction. I barely managed to pull myself together to get out the door with the proper pleasantries. Joe seemed fine as he backed his car out of the driveway and headed down the street to the first turn. But around the corner, he pulled over. We both had been felled by Amish hard cider. Joe slept in the front seat and I slept on the back seat for some unknown amount of time until Joe came to and decided he could make it back to Akron. And it was all for naught. Tom Gindlesberger voted with the railroads. The Riverlake Belt Conveyor was dead.

There was another big legislative defeat my first term. The surprising loser was Frank J. Lausche, who was then the governor. He seldom asked for legislation that wouldn't pass. Many thought him faithless to party and friends. He seemed to enjoy opposition, his own and others. Sometimes he even rewarded opponents with unexpected positions his friends had hoped for. But he was a consistent winner. I had no doubt of the source of his tremendous vote-getting power after I heard him present his "state of the State" address. I don't remember what it was about. Maybe it wasn't even important. But Lausche had a wonderful, warm, almost caressing way of saying "people."

Typically, it was "for the people" that Lausche called us back into a spe-

L to R: Thomas L. Thomas, me, and Governor Frank J. Lausche, 1955.

cial session long after the regular session had ended. He asked us for the power to seize General Telephone Company, which was caught up in a long, bitter, violent strike that was causing serious hardship. The Taft-Hartley Act needed to be considered, however. Still fairly new, it regulated labor relations broadly at the federal level. On the advice of Senator Taft's son, Bob, a freshman member from Cincinnati, and several other lawyers of considerable note, our committee concluded that the Taft-Hartley Act as passed by Congress had preempted the field of state action in labor disputes. That being so, we couldn't pass the governor's bill. The tough job was to tell the governor. Several of us went to his office, but no one wanted to speak up. We sat there dumbly for a long time while the governor looked into our eyes, one by one. When someone finally gave him the bad news, he studied us all again with the wordless grief of one betrayed, then stood and nodded dismissal.

In only five years in the legislature, I served under four governors: Lausche, Brown, O'Neill, and DiSalle. Brown? When Lausche was elected to the United States Senate in 1956, he took office a few days before his term as governor expired (as George Voinovich did in 1999). That made Lieutenant Governor John Brown of Medina the governor. It was only for a short time, but Brown, a handsome, debonair former state highway patrolman, made the most of it, even finding time to address the legislature where he humorously complained that Senator Lausche must have slipped back into town because Brown's parking space in the statehouse was occupied by Lausche's shabby old car that morning. But the funny part was that it was not the senator but a custodian who had presumed to park in the governor's place. When someone told him, Brown didn't find that a bit amusing. Rodney Dangerfield would have understood his feeling.

The incoming governor a few days later was C. William O'Neill who had been Ohio's attorney general. He already had a reputation for surrounding himself with a bright group of young people, and he soon gained credit for the high caliber of appointments to his cabinet, boards, and commissions. He was also Ohio's last governor with a two-year term, because the Ohio Constitution called for four-year terms beginning in 1958. All O'Neill had to do was stay popular for two years, and then he could be elected for four years. That was his goal, and his prospects looked good. Costs were going up, but he had enough of the surplus built up during World War II in the Ohio treasury to meet the costs of those first two years. Still, he failed to win election to the succeeding full term. My impression was that he was trying to play it safe and got too cautious. The best thing I remember is that white lines were painted on the edges of highways for the first time. The worst thing I remember was that he signed a bill increasing fees for county services, and then, when protests rose, he retreated and signed a bill repealing the increases. That wasn't terribly bad, but it gave the impression he was likely to yield to pressure on more important matters. As a result, he simply did not accumulate a sufficient reservoir of goodwill to sustain him when all those Democratic voters poured out in 1958 to defeat the right-to-work proposal on the ballot.

L to R: **Representative Thomas L. Thomas, me, Governor C. William O'Neill, and Senator Fred Harter, 1958.**

The winner in 1958 was Michael V. DiSalle, the former mayor of Toledo. He was lucky to be helped by those "no" votes on the right-to-work ballot issue because he was an unconventional winner, witty and self-deprecating, the kind of politician that voters had seldom seen since Lincoln until Adlai Stevenson came along and were only just beginning to see in John Kennedy. DiSalle was short but he was a little taller than C. William O'Neill, and he got a kick out of asking people for the first time in his life to vote for "the bigger man for the job." He had that good memory for names that politicians are supposed to have but seldom do. He met my father once in Akron. My father probably made the meeting memorable by bragging outrageously about me, but still, it was remarkable that Mike recognized my father a year later eating breakfast in a cafeteria in Columbus. My father almost choked on his cereal when the governor of Ohio came over and said "Hello, Mac."

Mike DiSalle did only a few things wrong, but they all had to do with taxes, and if there is one thing that people are touchy about it is taxes. Costs were continuing to rise, and the last of the wartime surplus had been used up under O'Neill. New tax revenues had to be found, and Mike found them. But he tried to minimize the burden of his proposed tax increases by distributing them over just about every tax in the Ohio Revised Code. This produced a seemingly unending succession of tax bills we had to pass and people had to read about. It reminded me of the postcard I got from my father when I was a child in camp. "The cat's fine," he wrote me. "We're cutting off its tail but only an inch at a time."

Time and time again, we had to gather our meager Democratic forces to pass those tax increases. We had only a slim majority, although our own Summit County delegation was all Democratic by then, with Thomas L. Thomas, Ed Flowers, and myself joined by Charles Madden and Betty Smith, widow of John L. Smith who had been a member the previous term but who had died unexpectedly. In those days before one-person-one-vote altered the arithmetic as well as the makeup of the House, there were 139 members, so 70 were needed to pass legislation. The Democrats had only 76, and by nature Democrats are freethinkers. Tell them they have to do something, and they get their backs up. Side bargains often had to be struck to get the votes needed for every new tax. As chairman of the Judiciary Committee, I was party to a few of those side bargains, setting bills for hearing that I could only hope would die.

It didn't help that DiSalle said from the start he wanted open meetings in his administration. That was all very well for him, and it was the kind of thing that newspapers loved. But for Democrats in the House, open meetings created all kinds of extra problems. We felt our caucuses had to be open, too. That meant they were fully attended by the newspapermen covering the General Assembly. And that also meant that members who loved publicity had a great deal to say on every issue, as well as members who gloried in public dissent. The real business, with the necessary accommodations to unite the opinions of our small majority, sometimes had to be done piecemeal in doorways and around corners.

What did help was having an outstanding Speaker, Jim Lantz of Lancaster, who picked up A. G. Lancione's old votes, with A. G.'s full concurrence, and the votes of most of the newcomers. I voted for Jim Lantz, and I moved my seat at last, but I still liked my old Cleveland friends and helped get Mike Sweeney and Hugh Corrigan of Cleveland appointed vice-chairmen of the Judiciary Committee, despite their loyal votes for Jim McGettrick.

Understandably, the Democrats were sometimes confused over their newfound preeminence. But the Republicans were sometimes confused too. Over in the Senate, Republican Stanley Mechem of Athens, the former majority leader of the Senate, accidentally referred to his own party as the majority one day. The Democrats couldn't let that go by. Charlie Carney of Youngstown rose to his feet immediately on the Democratic side of the aisle. "The gentleman from Athens forgets there has been an election," he said. "*We* are the majority." He spelled it out: "M-A-G-O-R-I-T-Y." Hoots, catcalls, and delighted jeers came from the good spellers on the Republican side of the Senate.

By then, that Senate Democratic majority included a good friend of mine, Oliver Ocasek, who defeated Senator Fred Danner, the longtime in-

Oliver Ocasek

cumbent, and thereupon joined Fred Harter in representing our district. Fred Danner, president of Danner Press in Akron, was a gruff man who ran against "the money tree the politicians think is financing their spending." It was a good line, but Oliver had a good line of his own. He won on the slogan "Ocasek is OK for the Senate." It wasn't his first try, however. His name was just "different" enough in Summit County to need time for acceptance. It was easy for me the first time I encountered his name in about 1947. He was a student at Kent State then, and I was a student at The University of Akron, and we were both delegates to a model legislature. Oliver was running for Speaker at the time. I heard rather than saw his name, and "O'Casey" is what I heard. As a good Irishman, he got my vote. Later, he got my vote over and over again on his merits.

Another Democratic addition to the Senate was John W. Donahey, the lieutenant governor on Mike DiSalle's ticket. John owned a good political name. He was the son of Vic Donahey, once the state auditor, who rode to fame and then to the governorship of Ohio by refusing to accept a twenty-five-cent charge for a potato on someone's expense account. Later, when he was governor, Vic Donahey sold the copper roof of the statehouse in another fit of economy. His concern for the taxpayer's dollar was considered to be a heritable trait, which was a good thing for John because, although he was a thoroughly likable man, he had no obvious qualification for public office. His greatest interest, indeed, was in a process he developed for freeze-drying poultry. Few people visited his office in the Senate without being tossed a rock-hard Cornish game hen, polished and a little dirty from handling. John had another great asset besides his father's good name. It was his wife Gertrude, and she often spoke for him at political events. When John died, his wife in her turn put the Donahey name to use and was elected state treasurer. Her route to public office might not inspire a high school civics class, but she was one of the best state treasurers Ohio ever had—and probably also the nicest.

The biggest issue for me in 1959 was a formula used in determining public utility rates. Bill Wasick, the public utilities commissioner of Akron, had persuaded me back in 1954, before I got to the legislature, that utility rates were too high in Ohio due to the statutory requirement to value utility property at its reproduction cost new, less observed depreciation. The alternative proposal was to value property at its net original cost. I found that a change in the formula, known as RCND, was being sponsored by Republican members in my first term and tagged along on the legislation. The proposal went nowhere, however, being opposed by most Republican members. When the Democrats got the majority in my third term, I joined with Democrats Vern Riffe and Seamus Kilbane in seeking to change the RCND formula and had some high hopes. But, although it was a plank in the Democratic state platform, not a word of support came from the governor's office. When I protested this hotly, Mike DiSalle was simply amused by what he called Irish temper. I told him he hadn't seen the half of it yet: I was half French. That moved him. "Heaven help us," he said. "My wife is half French." At the last minute, he supported the bill, but the support came too late to be helpful, and the bill failed.

Not even a Democratic majority could turn the tide on changing the utility rate-making formula. We couldn't even get the bill out of committee until some arms were twisted. It was over this issue that I got into a major scrap with Thomas L. Thomas. We were otherwise tolerably good friends, but he refused to vote either for or against the bill in committee when we needed his vote, and I accosted him furiously after the committee meeting and said a few words. That led Tommy to complain in a letter to Mike DiSalle that I had threatened him. He said I told him if I had a knife I would stick it in his belly and cut out his guts. When Clyde Mann saw the letter and told me this, I was horrified. I said, "You *know* I wouldn't use language like that! What I really said was that if I had a knife I would *kill* him!" Clyde reported that "lesser" threat in the *Akron Beacon Journal* with some amusement. He also reported that Tommy complained in the same letter that he had been treated unfairly by Democratic leader A. G. Lancione when Tommy proposed an amendment during debate on the bill. Lancione, Thomas said, "made the worst booboo of his life by making a motion that Author Thomas and his amendment be laid on the table." This complaint caused great merriment and no less so when Lancione gravely denied moving to table Thomas.

Partway through my third term, I went to the governor's office to recommend Akronite Dick Tobin for appointment to the Ohio Industrial Commission—the same Dick Tobin, now an old friend, who was running for mayor of Akron in 1949 when I got started in politics above the Backstage Bar.

"Why don't you speak for yourself, Fran?" the governor asked. "Me?" I said. "I'm not interested in the Industrial Commission."

"What would interest you?" Mike asked.

I said, "Nothing I can think of except, maybe, the Public Utilities Commission."

Where that came from, I don't know. It was the first time I had ever thought of that, but it wasn't a bad idea. Not long after that, Mike offered to appoint me to the Public Utilities Commission after the session of the legislature wound up. Actually, I wasn't appointed until the following January, in 1960, because I had voted for a salary increase for the commission in my second term that made me ineligible to serve until one year after that term ended. (Bob Reider of Port Clinton was appointed to serve in the interval.)

I left the legislature with some real pangs. I had never done anything before that I liked so much, and I seldom liked anything so much again. But a Democratic majority was unlikely again for a while, and I knew the legislature would never again be so fulfilling. I was the only member to get a unanimous vote from newsmen choosing the "Outstanding Members of the House." Almost all my bills passed. I quit on top.

Near the end of the session, my mother came to visit the legislature for the first time. She loved seeing everything for herself and meeting all the people I had talked about. "Thank you for being so good to Frances," she told everyone she met. "Mother, not everyone was so good," I said to her. But when the legislature had adjourned and I took the appointment to the commission, with all the bad times forgotten and all the good times remembered, I said, without words but with a long backward look, "Thank you." To everyone.

Eleven The Public Utilities Commission

It was hard to leave Akron, even though I would be coming home every weekend. My mother had died unexpectedly not long after her visit to the legislature. We felt the loss every day, and my father was going to be left all alone when I went to Columbus. Since he didn't believe in cooking or cleaning, I didn't know how he would get along. He agreed, however, to settle for a Sunday roast or a meatloaf to see him through until Friday. He also tried to help by eating his meals on small plates. By the weekends, tippy stacks of saucers were piled high beside the kitchen sink. The doors of my law office also closed behind me. I had only a small practice, but I was proud of my association with John Quine, whom I greatly admired and liked. I never ceased to be grateful that he put up with me and my erratic political schedule when our old firm broke up after Clarence Motz's death in 1955.

What I was least prepared for was my friendlessness in Columbus in those first days. I had lived in a virtual neighborhood at the corner of Broad and High Streets when the legislature was in session. Between the hotel and the statehouse, I might say a dozen hellos to members, lobbyists, and visitors from home. But they all disappeared when the session was over. And when I was no longer staying at the hotel, there wasn't even Wilbur, the bellman, to say hello or goodbye.

After I found an apartment on one of the few hillsides around Columbus, however, I didn't miss Akron so much, and I liked the Public Utilities Commission from day one. There were three members in those days, with six-year terms. I was serving the tag end of a term, having been appointed to fill a vacancy. (Now there are five commissioners with five-year terms.)

The chairman, appointed by Governor Mike DiSalle, was Edward J. Kenealy, an engineer who used to run the Cleveland municipal electric system back when it was functioning as a system. His wiry build, ruddy complexion, and puffs of white eyebrows seemed to go with his edgy, light sense of humor. He was not a man easily impressed or taken in by eminence or au-

Being sworn in as a Public Utilities Commissioner by Governor Michael V. DiSalle, 1960.

thority. The other commissioner was Everett Krueger, one of the best of C. William O'Neill's appointments. He was big enough to make two of Ed, but he always deferred to Ed with an inborn courtesy and warmth to match Ed's sharp-edged wit. He also had a very extensive vocabulary that he used when he talked, as well as when he wrote.

The three of us got along very well but didn't always agree on outcomes. Ed used to accuse Everett and me of being legalistic, and we accused him of oversimplifying. If we split, it was sometimes along party lines, but often our decisions were unanimous, although I remember that when Everett was going to write one of our opinions, I said, only half-jokingly, that if it had more than one "ergo" in it, I would dissent.

Within a few days after I arrived, I was initiated into an important ritual. Our office was on the first floor of the State Office Building—the only one that existed in 1960, yellow brick and Art Deco on Front Street, a block from the capitol. Across a splendid hall was a splendid hearing room, about twenty feet high, dimly lit and echoing, with one of those Depression Era murals full of gears, blue shirts, and biceps, and with an imposing high bench for the commission. Beginning in the reception room of our offices, Ed Kenealy would line the three of us up in the order in which we would sit on the bench—Everett first, Ed in the middle as the presiding officer, and then me. Everett could never resist some pleasant remark as our ranks formed, and I could never resist some gleeful response. Ed waited until we had achieved a decorous silence. Then, with a last check on our alignment, he gave the order to march. The receptionist held the door open and ran ahead to open the hearing room door across the hall, and march we did, across, through, and up into our places. Participants stood politely until we were seated. Ed then called the case to order.

What we were hearing most of the time were applications by gas, electric, water, and telephone companies to increase rates. These cases were brought infrequently and decided slowly, probably far too slowly, but they involved millions of dollars and mountains of testimony on issues of engineering, accounting, economics, finance, and law. I had expected to be ignorant, not uncomprehending, but for a long, long time I ran a full paragraph or more behind on everything being said. A witness might say, for example, "The usage would necessarily affect load factor." I'd be thinking: Load? Load

L to R: me, Martin Galvin, secretary of the Commission, Edward J. Kenealy, and Everett Krueger on the Public Utilities Commission bench, 1960.

factor? Affect how? Why necessarily? By then the speaker would be developing another point.

Each utility also had its own arcane vocabulary. Glossaries helped on the hard terms. It was ordinary English used in unexpected ways that was more likely to trip me up—telephones referred to as "stations," "equipments" used in the plural, "demand" and "energy" in new contexts, and so forth. We also regulated most intrastate trucking and the service and safety of railroads. After distinguishing between regular and irregular routes and certificated versus contract carriers in the trucking industry, I was glad to find that a few terms, such as "balloon freight," meant what they appeared to mean. But the only new language I really liked was the colorful language of the railroads, where "gandy dancers" worked on the tracks and "telltales" brushed the shoulders of trainmen on the roofs of cars to warn them of a low bridge or tunnel entrance ahead.

For the most part, the commission supported itself through fees levied on the utilities it regulated, so it was considered better able to pay rent than most state agencies. That meant, with DiSalle's penny-pinching, that we soon had to leave our free marble precincts for a rented space. We moved the July after I arrived, but not before my friend Bernie Rosen came visiting from Akron and observed I was reading between the lions. It was perceptive of him to notice that, I said. "No, no," Bernie said. "Li-ons!" Sure enough, two stone lions were couchant outside my windows. There would be nothing so imposing at our new offices in a remodeled dime store on North High Street, but we were not without resource. The former storefront had been filled in with a facade marked "Public Utilities Commission of Ohio" in big letters and adorned with an aluminum casting of the Great Seal of Ohio. Many people have lions, but how many have seals? When we gathered out front for the dedication, I said, "I thought I heard a seal bark." People looked at me uneasily. Evidently the caption of James Thurber's cartoon of a seal in the bedroom wasn't as famous as I thought it was, not even in Thurber's hometown.

An interesting feature of my appointment to the commission was that it was a first. As late as 1960, I was the first woman to be appointed to a utility regulatory commission, state or federal. Now these appointments are common, and indeed a woman with the wonderful name of Peaches Brown was appointed to West Virginia's utility commission soon after, and she went on to serve on the Interstate Commerce Commission, a first at the federal level. In the interval of more than fifty years between the shock to men of women's suffrage and the assault of women's liberation, only a few good positions were available to women. But it was a sweet interval for some of us with an early start in politics. The late Margaret Spellacy was a judge of the juvenile court in Cuyahoga County. Once after she or I or both of us were honored in some fashion, we acknowledged conspiratorially to each other that, while we might advocate wider recognition for women, we didn't mind being in a small group when the choice was about to be made for some nice appointment or recognition.

Few women appreciated being treated as pariahs in men's clubs or banished to flowered curtains and salad lunches in the ladies' dining rooms. The Columbus Athletic Club permitted women in the main dining room for dinner only. The more exclusive Columbus Club, in a charming, old-fashioned brick house with an iron fence and green lawn near the statehouse, permitted women to enter only through a side door leading up a staircase directly to a private dining room. The first time I was invited to lunch there, I came in the front door, not knowing any better. I have never forgotten the flapping arms as horrified men rose like bats from their deep chairs and shooed me back out the door. Many years later, I was told that no woman had ever crossed the threshold of the club's front door. "I did," I said with great satisfaction. In Pittsburgh, the rule at the Duquesne Club was no women through any door in daylight. I was smuggled in once on a freight elevator for lunch in a back room. I would have preferred to eat somewhere else.

There were other unheralded breaches of the rules. In 1961, Ohio Bell

Telephone permitted me to take the place of one of their own employees at a weeklong annual course on utility financing given by John Childs, a vice president of the Irving Trust Company at One Wall Street in New York. Besides lectures and role-playing, we also had some memorable excursions. One was to the vault of the Federal Reserve Bank, where we could observe men with hard-toed shoes wheeling gold ingots about to settle international trade accounts. Another excursion was to the floor of the New York Stock Exchange, to which, at that time, women were never admitted. I understood I would have to watch from the balcony and made no complaint, but since I was the first woman to take the course, this came as a surprise to John Childs, and he was unwilling to accept it. At the last moment, I was told to go in with the rest of our group of about twenty. I was assigned to a specialist who made the market in Brown Shoe Company stock. He not only enjoyed breaking the rules with me but even let me give some quotations. My visit was, however, an unacknowledged exception. Several years later, Queen Elizabeth visited the floor of the New York Stock Exchange. The newspapers reported that she was the first woman ever to do so.

Akron City Club has had women members since 1978, after the new Cascade Club embarrassed it with an open-door policy. But even before then, it was always generous with exceptions. I had many bar association lunches in the main dining room, and if I wished to take someone to lunch—in the ladies' dining room—on business, I simply "borrowed" a membership. When the time came, I was one of the first women members. I was also on the board in 1985. By then, the board was more concerned about chefs and corkage fees than gender.

Being a first at the Public Utilities Commission didn't mean there was any reluctance to share out the work. All three of us heard the rate cases at length after a staff investigation and report, although we relied on attorney-examiners to hear customer complaints and cases regarding railroads and trucking, and we usually adopted the examiners' findings. Regulation used to be much more inclusive and extensive. Nobody thought of encouraging competition. The whole idea was to regulate monopolies to achieve economies of scale, reasonable rates, reliability, and service without discrimination. At least this was so for gas, electric, water, and telephone companies. This meant we regulated rates, service, accounting, and security issuances.

It was also assumed that the commission and its investigative staff, acting as fact finders, should be able to balance fairly the interests of customers and utilities. In a few cases, municipalities intervened on behalf of local customers. Bill Wasick, Akron's utility commissioner, was a regular and welcome intervenor. But there was no Consumers Counsel. The staff was the adversary when staff findings were challenged by the utilities. To an unseemly extent, the commissioners also acted as adversaries. We were supposed to be impartial judges, but sometimes the only way to get at the facts was by cross-examining witnesses. To minimize this, we asked Andy Sarisky, an assistant attorney general assigned to the commission, to do some of the questioning. Many years later, when I returned to the commission as an attorney for Ohio Edison Company, I found the assistant attorneys general considered us the enemy. I shouldn't have been surprised.

I would say we were happy (some 150 of us) in our new dime-store offices. They were clean and bright, and there were nice allowances for new furniture. Unfortunately, we ran a little low on funds when we got to the hearing rooms. After buying three big, comfy swivel chairs for ourselves in the main hearing room, there was little money left for chairs for participants. Martin Galvin from Toledo, the secretary of the commission, solved the problem by finding inexpensive stackable plastic chairs on wire frames. But "Orange?" every person said on seeing them. The color apparently had a lot to do with the price, so orange it was. We probably had the gaudiest hearing rooms in state government.

The witnesses were not gaudy, but sometimes they were exceptional. One such was a man with a squawky voice, a long neck, and a small head that he turned with birdlike dips and swivels. He was Dr. W. Edwards Deming. I couldn't take my eyes off him. A statistician, he testified on sampling in a battle between Ohio Bell and General Telephone Company. Astonishing as his manner was, it compelled confidence—and it must have had the same effect on others. He later became a cult figure in the field of industrial management, particularly in Japan, and, although he died in 1993 at the age of ninety-three, his approach to achieving quality assurance and customer satisfaction continues to have an impressive following, judging by a dozen or more Web sites devoted to Deming.

In my first year at the commission, however, I had much more than hearings and new ideas to capture my attention. The most exciting presidential campaign of the century was about to begin in 1960, and I got to enjoy some of the excitement.

Twelve "Kennedy Will Win"

We were all still guessing who would emerge as the Democratic candidate for president in 1960 when I was asked late in 1959 to be on the slate of Ohio delegates-at-large to the Democratic National Convention, pledged to Governor Michael V. DiSalle as favorite son. It took me no longer to say yes than to say yes. It was an honor to be asked, and no campaigning would be required because voters would choose the slate, not the individuals.

Of course, real candidates for president could oppose DiSalle by running their own delegates in Ohio, but the conventional wisdom was that a serious candidate for president would do better to win the ultimate support of a favorite son and his delegates than to incur his ill will and maybe lose some delegate races. As for the commitment to a favorite son, the conventional wisdom was that it kept delegates together until a likely winner emerged who would properly appreciate the votes with jobs, preferments, and so forth.

Jack Kennedy wasn't constrained by conventional wisdom. He was a front-runner, but by all accounts he didn't think he could win the nomination from a brokered convention. Thus he felt he had to secure his own votes in advance and then win on the first ballot, the only ballot for which commitments were solid. When a preliminary survey indicated he would need all of Ohio's sixty-four votes, the choice was to run his own delegates or to persuade Mike DiSalle to back him from the start. According to Kennedy's aide Ted Sorensen in *Kennedy,* his account of Kennedy from his first days in Congress, DiSalle was "flirting" with Senator Stuart Symington of Missouri. That may or may not have been true, but it was enough to cause Kennedy to consider running his own delegates in Ohio where he was showing well in polls and could expect an endorsement from the *Cleveland Press.* That prospect, in turn, was enough to persuade DiSalle to pledge his delegates to Kennedy even before Kennedy made his formal announcement of candidacy in early January 1960. I had some misgivings about Kennedy; I felt drawn to him but remembered all the stories of anti-Catholicism bred by Al Smith's candidacy. Already the old joke had been revived that when Smith lost, he sent the Pope a one-word telegram: "Unpack." For me, DiSalle's decision was a relief. I didn't have to argue with myself. I could go where my inclinations were taking me.

If DiSalle's pledge to Kennedy was all that happened, I could still have run statewide on his at-large slate, but two events took me to the local ballot instead. First, Ray Miller, the county chairman of Cuyahoga County, seeing the advantage of being with Kennedy, apparently decided to run his own slate of delegates for Kennedy, with Albert Porter of Cleveland, Cuyahoga County's county engineer, as favorite son. Miller fielded only one delegate in our Fourteenth Congressional District, but it was Mary McGowan, my old nemesis. Her alternate, Bertha Moore, a friend of mine but no friend of Mike DiSalle's, was a leader in the Second Ward and the black community. Second, Anne Eaton, wife of Cleveland industrialist Cyrus Eaton, wanted to be a delegate. The Eatons lived in Summit County and were generous contributors to the Democratic party. But Cyrus Eaton was controversial—almost, one could say, notorious—because of his efforts at rapprochement with Nikita Khrushchev. Lingering McCarthyism would almost surely prevent his wife's election from Summit County.

And so it came to pass that Anne Eaton took my safe place on the statewide ballot, and I ran at home for delegate on the DiSalle ticket with Leo Berg, the mayor of Akron. Bob Shuff, a well-liked local lawyer with a strong labor background, and Leo Walter, a businessman long active in the party, were our alternates. I hated having to run on the local ticket. None of my friends in Columbus knew that I had lost twice to Mary McGowan, so there was no point in moaning there about my chances, but I could easily imagine losing and was overcome with chagrin at the prospect. Fortunately, I liked Anne Eaton, so I didn't blame her. She would have been hard to dislike, being blessed, it appeared, with a happy disposition, despite having had polio that left her confined to a wheelchair (except when she could swim in the superwarm outdoor pool back of the Eaton's house in Sagamore Hills).

She diplomatically invited Catherine Turner and me to lunch at her house one day in early spring. We expected to be impressed with signs of great wealth, but she disarmed us with flowered chintzes and old rugs. We didn't see the most famous souvenir of the Eatons' visits to Russia—a troika and the three horses to draw it, given to the Eatons by Khrushchev—but one wall of the living room was almost covered by an oil painting in the heavy style favored by the Soviet Union. Anne explained that her husband had admired it, and it was promptly given to them. The old saw "Be careful what you wish for" was worth remembering when they were traveling behind the Iron Curtain as the Soviet Union's only American friends. It wasn't until we were leaving that we also saw a fearsome boar's head, with tusks, bristles, and wild, glassy eyes, mounted on the wall above the front door— the souvenir of a Russian hunt. Anne liked the boar, but she said she thought she'd better put it inside the door so it wouldn't scare off arriving guests.

In March 1960, between the Wisconsin primary won by Hubert Humphrey and the West Virginia primary won by Kennedy, came my first thrills of the campaign. I went to a Midwest Conference in Detroit put on by the Democratic National Committee. The conference ran the entire weekend of March 26th, but a good indication of my commitment by then is that I can't remember anything at all of that weekend that didn't involve Kennedy, not even how I got there or the name of our hotel. I saw him first at a press conference, sitting down at a table across from newspapermen, answering questions easily, as if in discussion with friends. Today one would say "media" rather than "newspapermen," but "newspapermen" was still a more appropriate term at that time. There may have been some people there from news magazines, radio and television, and women as well as men, but not many. There certainly were no television lights and cameras.

Then came a Jefferson-Jackson Day dinner, attended by thousands. It was meant to be a showcase of candidates and there were six in the race by that time: Kennedy, Humphrey, Symington, Henry M. "Scoop" Jackson of Washington, Robert Meyner of New Jersey, and Lyndon Johnson. (Adlai Stevenson was awaiting another draft.) All the declared candidates were represented at the dinner, but not necessarily in person. Sam Rayburn, Speaker of the House, was there to speak for Johnson, his fellow Texan, and Senator Eugene McCarthy of Minnesota was there to speak for his compatriot Hubert Humphrey.

John Bailey of Connecticut, the chairman of the Democratic National Committee, was in charge. He was pretty well known to be for Kennedy, but he had to be fair, or at least look fair, in deciding the order in which the candidates or their representatives would speak, so he announced the order of speakers before dinner and explained how carefully this had been decided. When Kennedy nevertheless ended up in the favored last position, the audience laughed good-humoredly but a little skeptically.

At that moment, no one gave any particular importance to the second-to-last position, which went to Eugene McCarthy, who was going to be speaking for Hubert Humphrey. But after several ordinary speeches by the others, Eugene McCarthy took everyone by surprise with a magnificent speech that simply overwhelmed us. We shouted. We clapped. We rose to our feet in tribute. The applause went on and on. And Kennedy had to follow this.

Finally, the applause lightened enough to allow John Bailey to introduce Kennedy. Kennedy began by saying the only thing that was appropriate for that moment. He said, "I wonder if we aren't backing the wrong man for president." It was perfect. The applause broke out again, but now it was for the graceful response that acknowledged McCarthy's singular eloquence—and at the same time reminded us that McCarthy was not a candidate. Part of what made Kennedy special was this ability to sense what an occasion required.

I had met Kennedy and Jacqueline Kennedy a year before when Kennedy spoke at our local Jefferson-Jackson Day dinner, but a meeting with someone famous is always a little one-sided. I mean, I met Kennedy but he didn't exactly meet me. I got a second chance in Detroit. On Sunday morning, the day after the dinner, I was standing in front of the hotel with Marguerite Parrish of Dayton when Kennedy came out alone. It must have been one of the last times ever that he was alone, and it was only for a moment, because Marguerite and I stepped forward and I said, "We're two of Mike DiSalle's delegates." That would have been enough for most candidates, but Kennedy asked us our names and repeated them after us. By then, he had aides around him. A car drew up at the curb for him, and he was gone. But that afternoon, Marguerite and I went early to a reception for Kennedy and were standing inside, away from the long lineup, by a pair of mirrored side doors when the doors opened and Kennedy and his party came in beside us. "Hello again," he said to me, "and you too, Marguerite." Marguerite was almost carried away with excitement. She said, "He knows our names!" I didn't mind believing it, but I wasn't so sure he knew mine. Many times when I was campaigning for myself, I met several people at once and remembered only the last name I heard. Hanging on to that last name, I would try to get back to the same people before I left. After looking at everyone else and saying how nice it was to meet them, I would then turn to the only one whose name I remembered and add, "And you too, (whoever)." The reaction was usually like Marguerite's. They thought I remembered all their names.

When the May primary came along, Ray Miller won only seven and a half of Ohio's sixty-four delegates. I was relieved to find I came in first for delegate in our district, with 21,979 votes, leaving Mary McGowan well behind me with 13,540 votes. I was out of Mary's long shadow at last. Leo Berg came in second with 17,974 votes. But it was what lay ahead of me that was keeping me excited.

The Democratic National Convention was to be held in Los Angeles the week of July 11, 1960. It would have been wonderful enough just to be a delegate, but I was also on the Democratic National Platform Committee which began hearings at the Biltmore Hotel on the Tuesday before the convention began. Someone had come up with the idea that there should be a man and a woman from each state, and I was there with James White Shocknessy. Shocknessy, famous in Ohio as the head of the Ohio Turnpike Commission, was fun to be around. He was a big, burly, humorous man who used unexpected expressions like "My goodness" and even "My goodness me!" I confess I thoroughly enjoyed his full-voiced reaction to proposals from various speakers: "Incredible!" "Did you ever!" and so on. But, sitting next to him in the third tier of seats in the ballroom of the Biltmore Hotel, I pretended I didn't hear him when the speakers looked up indignantly. I did almost chime in with him once, however, when a rosy Irishman from Boston wanted a plank supporting a united Ireland. I had some sympathy with that view but not for the Sinn Fein and certainly not in a party platform.

I almost had Harry Truman on the other side of me. A week before, he had come out angrily against Kennedy (oddly, considering his own history, because of Kennedy's lack of experience) and he decided not to come to the convention. He was to have been on the platform committee and I was told a newspaper photograph showed his name placard beside mine at an empty table. Too bad. I imagined my side of a conversation: "You probably remember me from when I met you and your wife at a Democratic dinner in Cleveland in 1955 where you were the speaker." (I also imagined his response: "No.")

I was already settled into my hotel before the committee convened, but I walked to the Biltmore each morning for breakfast, glad to leave my hotel behind. Since I was there a week ahead of the convention, I hadn't expected a welcome committee, but I certainly also hadn't expected my cab to sweep up to a second-rate hotel and to find the small lobby lined with senior citizens being moved out to make room for the Ohio delegation. As the first interloper, I got the full bale of their baleful looks. My God, I thought. Ohio must have gone for Eisenhower in 1956! Nothing less awful could explain our Ohio headquarters, the Hotel Figueroa, located in a wind-swept or renewal-swept wasteland with only a few one-story establishments such as body repair shops, fortune-tellers, and stucco insurance offices. My room was perfectly clean but had a worn rug, wooden floor, gauze curtains, and old-fashioned roller window shades. There have been a few occasions when I have been impressed by my own importance. The Figueroa Hotel kept me from any vainglory in Los Angeles.

I guess it stands to reason that while a platform committee listens to proposals and even discusses them, as we did on Saturday after a week of hearings, it is others who write the platform—and well in advance. In fact, we thought it was theatrics when we were given a whole day off on Sunday by Chester Bowles, the chairman of the committee, to give the writers a chance to do their work. The platform arrived, fully printed, on Monday. Let it not be said we had no say-so, however. My own contribution on Saturday was a plank intended to favor metropolitan government. The written version did use the word "metropolitan" but was orthogonal at most, saying, "We propose 10-year action to restore our cities and provide for balanced suburban development, including Federal aid for metropolitan area planning and community facility programs." Bowles spoke at length on the need for a plank that called for ambassadors to know the language of the countries to which they were to be sent. We didn't mind being convinced. The plank was already printed.

There was only one big controversy. The civil rights planks were considered to be too strong by two delegates, Senators Holland of Florida and Eastland of Mississippi. They saw no need for new laws. If I remember right, it was Senator Holland who said no law could make him love his dear old Mammy more than he already did. That disarming form of resistance to civil rights was new to me, but I gather it was a song often sung before. Notwithstanding, we had no trouble accepting the civil rights proposals. One change did get made. An old gal from Pennsylvania named Emma Guffy Miller, whose brother had been a legendary senator, had evidently been on platform committees for years and years, and she noticed an omis-

Political Cartoon from 1960 Democratic National Convention.

sion in the 1960 draft. There wasn't a word about favoring the Equal Rights Amendment. "I thought I could stay home this time, but no, it's a good thing I came," she said in a furious, tight voice, and she pounded a good stout cane for emphasis. The usual plank on equal rights for women was quickly put back in the 1960 platform.

At first, I had killed time at the end of each day by roaming candidates' hospitality suites at the Biltmore. My favorite one was Stuart Symington's, presided over by two handsome and witty sons and well provided with refreshments. But it was in a small headquarters room for Kennedy that I came upon some very useful round stickers about four inches in diameter, red, white and blue, with Kennedy's picture in the middle. I took several back to the hotel. The Figueroa was livening up a little more each day as

Ohio delegates and guests arrived. My friends Bernie Rosen, Catherine Turner, and Ernie Teodosio were coming in as delegates-at-large and Leo Berg, Bob Shuff, and Leo Walter as local delegates like me. Ruth Rosen and Ralph Turner were also there, and so was the Reverend John Duffy and his family. Duffy, minister of the East Springfield Presbyterian Church in Ellet, was a big, tall Irishman from Boston and an ardent supporter of Boston's native son. Clyde Mann and Jim Jackson were also there for the *Akron Beacon Journal*. (John S. Knight, publisher of the *Beacon Journal*, was in town but was understandably staying at a different hotel.)

The convention didn't get going each day until late in the afternoon, prime time for television on the East Coast. That left us with time on our hands. We had different ways of killing the time. Bernie Rosen rented a car to take us to Hollywood one day. We had a short trip on a freeway. He got on all right but never made it to the through lanes. We were swept off at the next exit. Feeling a little silly, we made our way to Hollywood by way of a hundred or so traffic lights. Many Ohioans were basking each morning on the concrete shores of a little hotel pool, and that was one of my favorite spots. The most popular hangout was the hotel's dark little cocktail lounge, full most hours of the day. We were, of course, already committed to Kennedy on the first ballot, but there were many excited discussions over cocktails about whom to vote for on the second ballot. (We never dreamed of a first ballot victory.) Even people fiercely devoted to Kennedy joined the speculation, enjoying politics for the sake of politics, as politicians do.

On my floor, people had put up posters for Stuart Symington across from the elevators. That's where my stickers came in. The posters extolled his stellar qualities, but my stickers on the posters, which were peeled off each night by unknown hands but which I faithfully renewed each day, said what really counted. They said "Kennedy will win."

Thirteen **Electing Kennedy**

Delegates to the Democratic National Convention in the Los Angeles Sports Arena in 1960 needed three ears: one to listen to conversations and the hubbub around them, another to listen, or try to listen, to the speeches from the rostrum, and a third to follow Eleanor Roosevelt's movement from one section to another of the balcony above us. Each time she moved to a new section, there was a spontaneous rising up around her and the excited sounds of welcome. She was working the balconies for Adlai Stevenson.

But "Oh, no" was all I could think of Stevenson then. He was the past. This was the future. Most of us had been devoted to him when he ran in 1952 and 1956, but not even the second-ballot handicappers in our delegation considered him a candidate for nomination in 1960. He seemed to be a reluctant candidate, but he was probably encouraged to dream once again by the enthusiasm of California supporters who lay in siege at every portal to the convention. Catherine Turner and I had a disturbing view of him when he came to the convention floor as a delegate from Illinois. We had gone to the back of the arena for something cold to drink when we were slammed against the wall by a flying squadron carrying him through the crowd by his elbows, with his feet swinging a couple of inches above the floor. The violent wedge that parted the crowd seemed to leave him as frightened as the people being thrown to one side. His fear—and his freckles—are what stayed in my memory. I had seen him before on a campaign train that stopped in Elyria in 1952. How had I missed the freckles then?

My memory of Stevenson is curiously associated with another memory. In 1970, on a vacation trip to London, I stayed at the Grosvenor House Hotel near Grosvenor Square, where the American embassy is located. Stevenson had been walking in the square with his friend Marietta Tree when he died suddenly in 1965, and I had just seen a bronze plaque in the sidewalk marking the place. I sat down on a bench in the little park and probably was remembering him at the 1960 convention when a man came along walking a

whole flock of Pekingese dogs, five or maybe six. Their leashes were all attached to a ring, and when the man saw he had an audience on the park
bench, he dropped the ring to the ground. One Pekingese stepped up proudly, picked up the ring in her mouth, and ran forward, chin up, with a wedge
of lighthearted Pekes flying along behind her. How I do love that delightful
memory. To this day I can't remember Stevenson or the Pekingese without
remembering both.

Awaiting the first ballot on the convention floor, we worried ourselves
with questions. Would Governor Meyner release his New Jersey delegates to
Kennedy? Would Mayor Daley of Chicago permit his Illinois delegates,
mostly pledged to Kennedy, to vote instead, once again, for Stevenson, their
former favorite son? Could Carmine DiSapio of New York with his danger-
ous-looking dark glasses be counted on? Everyone was adding up votes, and
the totals kept changing. Lyndon Johnson's strategists conceded Kennedy
was in the lead but said he had crested too soon, and most counts showed
Kennedy with more like 741 votes than the 761 votes he needed to win on the
first ballot. The roll call of states would be read in alphabetical order, Alaba-
ma to Wyoming, when the time came for the various state delegations to
cast their ballots. If Kennedy didn't have a majority by the time West Virginia was called, most pundits thought a second ballot would be inevitable—and, for Kennedy, fatal because many commitments to Kennedy
were binding only on the first ballot.

Some in our own delegation were going to slip away on a second ballot
to Johnson or Symington. On the first ballot, however, we were all totally
loyal. Like a Kennedy fan club we all wore gold-washed PT 109 lapel pins
and "straw" boaters made of white plastic with red, white, and blue
Kennedy hatbands. If we owned anything red, white, and blue, we wore it. (I
wore a sleeveless white dress with appliqued red stripes.) Kennedy and Ohio
placards on long sticks were stockpiled beside us to be raised when Ohio
cast its vote.

And then at last the balloting began. People scratched over their tallies, adjusting estimates as the votes came in and counting even half votes with desperate earnestness. Kennedy was certainly piling up far more votes than the other candidates, but it looked for a while as if he were going to need the state of Xerxes, or even Zeno, to get the required 761 votes for a majority on the first ballot. When all but the votes of the very last state were still not enough to carry the day, there was a silence for the first time in the entire convention. And when the secretary of the convention called "Wyoming," one could hear a universal intake of breath. Wyoming saw its opportunity, and its split delegation came together. It cast all its votes for Kennedy and put him over with two votes to spare. The convention exploded. So, very nearly, did I. My ears popped. My shoulders ached. I felt like a racehorse who had stretched an impossible extra inch to win. We thought the world itself had won that night, and we had won the world.

After some prudent vote switching, the final first ballot total for Kennedy was 806. Now we had a long wait for Kennedy to come and accept our nomination. We heard he didn't want to come, that he wanted to save his

Catherine Turner, Margaret Mahoney, director of the Ohio Department of Industrial Relations, and Marguerite Parrish celebrating the nomination of Sen. Jack Kennedy at the 1960 Democratic National Convention.

words for his formal acceptance on the last night of the convention. But he had to give up and come anyway because no one would leave the arena until he did. We waited late into the night. Some filled the time by speculating on the choice for vice president. Most of us, however, were too wrung out with excitement to worry over what seemed only a detail then. Thank God, we didn't have a crystal ball that happy night. Thus we didn't see the choice of a vice president as a successor but only as whoever could bring the most votes to the ticket or, since we saw Kennedy uniquely as the strength of the ticket, for whoever wouldn't weaken it.

Mike DiSalle had already announced that he would nominate Symington for vice president if Kennedy won the nomination for president, but Kennedy chose Lyndon Johnson for vice president the next day. His pragmatism took us by surprise. He created the perfect match of northeast and southwest, but the styles and the history of Kennedy and Johnson were so unlike we had to shake ourselves to see them as a team. Mostly our surprise was that Johnson wanted the vice presidency. As majority leader of the Senate, he had far more power than a vice president, and he was a man who enjoyed power. Also, a failed candidate for the presidency didn't usually accept a nomination for vice president, although Estes Kefauver had done so in 1956. But what seemed politically unlikely when we first heard of it seemed like a master stroke on reflection. Kennedy gained the southwest, and Johnson, whatever he might be sacrificing, was gaining a national base for the future that he probably never could have gained otherwise in that period.

One thing we didn't doubt in our delegation was Johnson's ability to be president in his own right. He had sought a second-ballot vote from our Ohio caucus at the Figueroa Hotel a few days earlier, and most of us found him impressive as a candidate. What I remember better, however, is that he was impressively big, seeming to occupy the whole room with his presence. He also had more than a modest measure of what used to be called "animal magnetism." (By 1964, when I saw him again, he had lost that quality, due, I decided, to badly fitted teeth.) In accounts of the convention, liberals are said to have had misgivings about Johnson's southern roots, but most of us, unschooled in the nuances of polity, thought that if Johnson accepted the platform, including its civil rights plank, all would be well.

One who had notably supported Johnson, for president and anything he wanted, was the "Hostess with the Mostes'"—Perle Mesta. Incredibly, she gave a brunch for all of us in an arena-sized area of one of the Los Angeles hotels. The brunch had the biggest array of food I ever saw in one place, and waiters circulated constantly with trays of Bloody Marys and Orange Blossoms for any who had missed their morning juice or didn't mind having "seconds." We started out eager to see our celebrated hostess but missed her. After a few juices, we didn't care all that much.

On the last night of the convention, we sat up high in the Los Angeles Coliseum for the acceptance speech. It was full daylight when we arrived, and the evening darkened slowly, like houselights dimming for a great production. Two small planes flew a senseless pattern overhead. They were Republicans up there! We knew it! Trying to spoil our night! But as the twilight came, only one plane droned in the distance, seeming to deepen the night sky when Kennedy arrived below and stepped forward to speak, lit all alone in growing darkness. I have already said how he drew us out in asking us to give him our hand, our voice and our vote. But it was when he said, "The torch has been passed to a new generation of Americans," that I realized I and most of my friends had truly come of age and, moreover, that we had an obligation to serve some great cause.

That was what Kennedy uniquely brought to many of us—this sense of a role to play, a purpose to fulfill, however variously each of us defined that role and purpose. I read once that Kennedy, quoting some ancient sage, defined "happiness" in related terms. "Happiness," he said, "is the full use of one's powers along lines of excellence in a life affording scope."

Eight years after the convention, after Martin Luther King Jr. and then Robert Kennedy were killed, I was on an elevator in downtown Akron when two people were deploring Bobby's death. "But remember," one of them

said, "they said the world would come to an end when John Kennedy was as-
sassinated, and, look, we're getting along all right." "Oh, but are we?" I burst
out. For me, something that lifted me above myself that last night of the
1960 convention died when John Kennedy died.

I certainly had no immediate great purpose to serve, however, when the
convention ended. I stayed over a few days to visit an old friend and her family in Pasadena. We went to Disneyland, which was unique at that time, and
I also went to the Huntington Library. But I was still thinking convention. I
zipped by ephemera like the Gutenberg Bible and Gainsborough's famous
paintings of Pinkie and the Blue Boy at the Huntington, but I hung for a long
time over an exhibit of the journal of Thomas Haines Dudley, a delegate to
the 1860 Republican convention in Chicago, the convention that nominated
Abraham Lincoln. Of course, I resolved to preserve my own memories of the
1960 convention, already sure it was the convention of the century, an opinion I haven't changed. But it was a resolution I didn't keep. Major players
and historians have written chapters about the convention in books touching on the great issues, and I have read those books avidly. None, however,
can suggest how it was for someone who was just an excited delegate, con-
scious merely of a great sea change in politics. Except for a few notes in the
margins of accounts by others, my memories never got written down. All
that remains is what I have written here, many years later, and the
unerasable feeling that the event changed my life.

Fourteen Winning Ways

It wasn't clear for a while where I was going to have an opportunity to campaign. I was given a handmade American flag when I was named Ohio Democratic Woman of the Year in 1960, and I was eager to wave it, at least metaphorically, but all that came my way were a very few invitations to speak to Democratic clubs. I talked mostly about the national platform. Not surprisingly, audiences' eyes glazed. I even bored myself. Then Bill Coleman, the Ohio Democratic chairman from Marysville, and Helen Gunsett from Van Wert, Democratic national committeewoman for Ohio, rescued me by asking me to take the Kennedy women through Ohio—John Kennedy's mother, Rose, and two of his sisters, Pat Kennedy Lawford and Jean Kennedy Smith.

All three were to go to small cities in Ohio that wouldn't likely be reached by Kennedy himself. Columbus, where Rose Kennedy started, was the big-city exception. Rose Kennedy went on from there to Xenia, Warren, and Medina over three days. Seventy years old, thin as a spider, she looked her age, but she had a lovely, brief smile, and I admired her. I wasn't sure I liked her, however. Or rather, let me say, I liked her companions more. One was her maid, all smiles until she saw the way I packed my clothes. She showed me how to fold everything with tissue paper to avoid wrinkles. The other was Helen Hahn, a pretty, pleasant volunteer from Washington, D. C., whose family had a chain of shoe stores there. We became friends in common cause, so to speak: Rose Kennedy ignored us both.

She didn't ignore God, the hotel staff, or the press, however. To our astonishment, she got up early the first morning, went to Mass at the cathedral in Columbus, three good long blocks from the Deshler-Hilton Hotel where we were staying, and visited the kitchen help and the maids in the hotel basement before Helen and I even had our breakfasts.

She was an old hand with the press. Reporters had pretty much the same questions at every stop, so by the time she got to Ohio she had given the same answers many times before. "Did she see anything special in Jack when he was growing up?" All her children were special, she said. "How did she manage with nine children?" It wasn't difficult, she said, but she was afraid she'd forget who had what childhood illness so she kept records for each child on recipe cards.

She was also used to being photographed. She knew her best camera angle and arranged herself in advance very straight in a straight chair with a little fanny cushion behind her. The chair was always set so her head would be slightly turned when she faced the cameras. There was one small tangle in Akron, where she was staying for a few hours at the Sheraton Mayflower between her visits to Warren and Medina. The only reporter to come for an interview was Betty Jaycox from the *Akron Beacon Journal* who was kept in the outer room for a long time before we realized Mrs. Kennedy was waiting for the rest of the reporters to arrive before inviting them to come in. When we explained the peculiarity of having only one newspaper, she agreed to see Betty. But then Betty failed to ask about how she kept track of her children, so she had to volunteer the information. I don't think she was happy. As for Helen and me, this was the fourth time we heard about the recipe cards. Even good stories don't bear repeating more than once.

Someone else was unhappy in Akron: Mayor Leo Berg. He wanted to ride with Mrs. Kennedy to Medina, just fifteen miles away. That was reasonable and not a bit presumptuous, but one of the ground rules for all of the Kennedy women was that they didn't want any local dignitaries riding with them. The problem for me was that I was the one who had to impart this piece of bad news to Leo. He not only took it badly, but he was sure this was my personal ruling, although it is hard to see what I could have gained from it, while I would have gained a great deal if I had been able to get him in the limousine. In a way, I was adding insult to ignominy because another rule was that they wanted sheriffs, not local police, to provide escort services. Summit County's sheriff delightedly rode shotgun in Akron in a car conspicuously marked with his name, leaving the Akron police with nothing to do but watch.

There were other troublesome rules. One had to do with ropes. Nowadays we read about candidates and other dignitaries "working a rope line," but in 1960 the candidates just worked the crowd. The Kennedy women did want ropes, but they wanted to stand behind a rope themselves at their receptions, and far enough behind that guests had to lean far forward to shake their hands. Probably this was an old idea related to security, but it was new to us at the last moment before the first visit. We had an anxious colloquy among ourselves about what was being sought, and we decided that a velvet-covered rope between heavy stanchions such as we had seen in theaters would meet requirements. But evidently it was a rare theater that had one. After several increasingly urgent calls, we finally located a funeral director in Columbus who had something like what we were after. He lent it to us, but just for Columbus, so an anguished search for a rope line had to be made for the next stops. We wanted to leave it to the local committees to find one, but we couldn't count on their success. Finally, someone contrived an inelegant solution: clothesline strung through ringbolts on two-by-two-inch posts. We'd probably have to locate some marine rope if we were doing this today. Who has a clothesline?

The other rule was no chairs. "The aged?" we asked. "The infirm?" The campaign committee was adamant. This rule created a phenomenon. Chairs might not be set out, but they appeared anyway as if by magic. This couldn't be put down to defiance. The local committees were as disbelieving as we were when we passed the rule along, but they were willing to abide by it. The guests, however, were sure the absence of chairs was an oversight, so they produced their own. Matters reached a critical pass in Portsmouth, where a reception was held for Jean Kennedy Smith. The committee followed the rule, but, at the last minute, the hotel manager undertook to correct what he was sure was a mistake. When I saw the chairs going up around the perimeter of the reception room, I persuaded the manager to fold the chairs away in a big storage cupboard in the foyer, and not only that, but to lock the cupboard and take the key away with him. The reception was hardly under way, however, before I saw guests beginning to come through the line with chairs in hand. I raced for the foyer. There I saw an incredible sight—the guests lining up at the open storage cupboard to receive chairs like tickets of admission. I tried to explain the rule, but who was I? They smiled tolerantly, but they never broke step as they took their chairs, one by one, and went inside.

I liked Pat Lawford and Jean Smith. Both of them came in with companions from school days, and they seemed to be enjoying themselves. Pat Lawford shared her mother's predilection for early-morning walks. I think it was in Elyria that she and her friend, both good-looking and very tall, went striding down the street at the crack of dawn. They must have been a stunning sight. Several astonished followers came back with them. I confess I didn't see them myself, not being given to early rising or walks. I was given to vicarious vertigo, however, and when Pat Lawford got a call from Peter Lawford while we were with her I thought, Imagine! Peter Lawford almost in the same room with us!

Much as I liked Jean Kennedy Smith, who was about my age, I was thoroughly put out with her the day we traveled from Portsmouth to Athens for a big reception scheduled for two or three o'clock. The two off-duty state highway patrolmen who were driving Jean and her companion were unfortunately at her beck and call, and she becked and called them all over southern Ohio. To use my all-time favorite legal phrase, they were "off on a frolic of their own," leaving the guests in Athens standing—well, sitting—for a couple of hours. Just as Pat Lawford shared her mother's predilection for early-morning walks, Jean Smith shared her mother's predilection for campaigning where she wasn't expected. I don't know everywhere they went, but Jean did explain that in one town they saw a lot of cars outside a bowling alley, so they went in. They not only worked the crowd there, they bowled. They arrived in Athens unrepentant and exhilarated by all the extra votes they had picked up along the way.

My last contribution to electing Kennedy was just to vote for him on election day. I left Columbus early and set out for home at a reasonable rate of speed, but on the only stretch of Interstate 71 completed at that time, between Mount Gilead and Route 224, I seemed to be the only car on the road, and I let the car find its own speed. It was too fast for a state highway patrolman, and he pulled me over. While he was checking my driver's license, I told him hopefully that I was on my way home to vote for Kennedy. The patrolman looked at me for a long moment. "Well, drive safely," he finally said with a smile, and waved me on.

Kennedy won, of course, but he didn't win in Ohio. I felt as if I had lost the election myself. But there was, at least, the inauguration to look forward to on January 20, 1961.

My invitation to the inauguration came in the mail a few weeks later, looking like an oversized wedding invitation. Next, we all got information on making hotel reservations at the Pick-Lee House assigned to Ohio. The memory of the Figueroa Hotel was still fresh, so I expected the worst of the Pick-Lee after our loss in Ohio but was assured that it was a perfectly nice hotel and well located. Either Ohio was forgiven for voting for Nixon, or, more likely, the hotel was assigned before the outcome was known.

Then came the invitation to the inaugural ball. That occupied all my thoughts for several weeks. Who would go with me? What would I wear? The matter of an escort worked itself out beautifully. I wasn't exactly close with my money, but I was, shall I say, frugal. Even supposing I could find someone willing to take a trip all the way to Washington to go to the ball, I wasn't eager to pay for a second expensive ticket. Fortunately, Bob Shamanski, later a congressman from Columbus, a very nice, single Democrat, was in the same situation—needing someone to take to the ball without any inordinate expense. Friends got us together.

The dress for the ball took more agonizing. I looked all over and couldn't find anything that didn't look like Mother of the Bride or Sweet Sixteen. But in the back of my closet was a pale pink strapless dress I wore (with a stole) as a bridesmaid in the wedding of my friends Alice O'Neil and Frank

Gaffney years before. No taffeta for that wedding! The dress of silk marquisette was beautiful and quite expensive. (I believe Alice subsidized part of the cost.) I had wanted a "dedicated" dress for the ball, but in the end I was glad to settle for what I had. And then I also needed a long winter evening coat. I had something left from college, a slightly moth-eaten bright red wool with gold braid. That wouldn't do at all. Again, I had good luck— indeed, better luck than I realized at the time of purchase. I found a full-length dark blue velvet coat with a hood, and the velvet was treated to repel rain. It turned out to be just what I was going to need for the unexpected wet snow that arrived the day before the inauguration. The snow added drama to the historic scene, but it tied up Washington traffic, including all taxis, and poured through the slits in the pavement downtown, shorting out the underground lines that served the streetcars.

Thanks to the snow, I put the long velvet coat to good use the night before the inauguration, as well as a pair of knee-high boots I had worn to Washington more for style than for utility. Dick Kirkpatrick, Washington correspondent for the *Cincinnati Inquirer*, whom I had known from my legislature days, had invited me to dinner at the National Press Club. Fortunately, it wasn't far from the Pick-Lee House, and when we realized there was no way to get a cab in the snowfall, I sloshed my way to the Press Club on foot, wearing my high boots and ankle-length velvet coat with my shoes in a bag. I was a sight, and I arrived shedding snow like a dog, but I was dry under my coat and hood.

I would have had to wear the long evening coat again in the cold weather the next day to watch the inaugural parade but for a wonderful invitation for all of us from Akron to see the parade from the second floor of the brokerage firm Ferris and Company, directly across the street from the Treasury Department on Sixteenth Street. It wasn't that Ferris and Company cared anything about us, but Julia Montgomery Walsh, a vice president, did. Julia was from Akron, and her mother, Margaret Curry of Goodyear Heights, was one of our group. Julia, known as Peg in Akron and at Kent State University, had passed the Foreign Service examination of the State Department on one try, an unusual achievement. After a short career in the State Department, she married a pilot. They had four young children when he was killed. To support them, Julia became a broker at a time when this was uncommon. She was notably successful. She later was president of the American Stock Exchange. Later also, she married a widower with several children of his own, and they had another child together. I once visited them in Washington, and half the fun of a delightful evening at Julia's house was seeing kids everywhere, seemingly all about the same age except for the baby.

Ferris and Company went all out for us. The length of the long room opened onto a balcony over Sixteenth Street for a perfect view of the parade. Equally attractive inside was a bar and immense repast, and inside is where we saw the swearing in on television. Actually, we spent most of our time inside, out of the raw wind. Our pleasure in our snug situation was probably heightened by the view from the balcony of the crowd huddled below. One person with puzzling proportions turned out to be sitting on a camp chair under a big blanket. We wondered how some of the children could see above scarfs tied over their faces, but they evidently could. We heard their happy squeals when drum majors and clowns did their tricks.

The weather was colder still that night, and the snow had stopped falling when friends of Bob Shamanski took us to the inaugural ball in their car. Better still, Bob's friends took us first to a cocktail party in Georgetown, across the street and only a short distance from where John and Jacqueline Kennedy still lived. We saw them leave from their house in Georgetown, in a long line of quiet cars, with no fanfare. Georgetown was almost as interesting as its residents, at that time. It was still being gentrified. Houses showing years of ruinous neglect still stood beside houses beautifully restored. The empty downstairs of the row house where we went to our cocktail party could be seen from the entry, stripped to the brick walls and lit by a couple of bare light bulbs hanging from the ceiling.

The ball was the last thrill of the "Kennedy year" in my life. We sat at long tables in tiers around the dance floor in a hall so vast I was reminded of the Moonlight Ballroom at Myers Lake under the stars. But at Myers Lake, we danced to Ray Noble, Stan Kenton, and other contemporaries. At the inaugural ball for the youngest president of my lifetime, we danced to an ancient society band with hokey rhythms that suggested New Year's Eve with Guy Lombardo more than the New Frontier with John Kennedy. It was enough, however, that we we were there. It was the ball of the century.

Fifteen **Unconfirmed Roomer**

The Public Utilities Commission was not as exciting as a presidential election, but I was enjoying myself—mostly, I'm sure, because of the people I was working with. These included not only my fellow commissioners, Ed Kenealy and Everett Krueger, and later their successors, Dale Fulton and Rankin Gibson, but also, among many others, the secretary of the commission, Martin Galvin from Toledo, a political appointee like me; Jim Fullin, the assistant secretary; Paul Hampton, the chief engineer; Bill Lindsay, an economist who was earning his doctorate in utility rate making at Ohio State University; Basil Boritski, a lawyer and mathematician who headed up the telephone section; Ed Skipton, an accountant; Fran Hull, my secretary; Andy Sarisky, an assistant attorney general; and a bright bunch of attorney examiners, eventually including Jim Davis, my old friend and former Senate page, after he finished law school. I think I laughed more in those early days at the commission than at any other time in my life. Marty Galvin, secretary of the commission, was born to be funny and was also a great appreciator of everyone else's humor. His big peals of laughter from the office across the hall would set me off even when I didn't have any idea what he was laughing about.

Another reason I was enjoying the commission was that I was learning a lot. It wasn't knowledge I could apply elsewhere or even brag about, but it made issues interesting. Even simple subjects like depreciation could open up major issues of policy. One early issue, for example, was whether to give present utility customers the benefit of income tax savings produced by accelerating the tax deduction for depreciation in the early years on an item of property. Later deductions would be commensurately lower, of course, so taxes would be higher in later years on the same item of property. In rate-making terms, the choice was to "flow through" the tax benefit to present customers or to save it, that is, "normalize" the depreciation deduction, for the benefit of future customers. The commission of my day elected to flow through the benefit, after concluding that future tax liability for depreciation on the property of growing companies would never catch up to the present savings.

I had already discovered in the legislature that I liked working with figures. That didn't improve my arithmetic, however, and I was particularly bad at decimal points—no small matter in cases dealing with millions of dollars. I learned to keep my calculations to myself. I wasn't above faking a facility with figures during hearings by zipping up and down a seven-inch slide rule, but about all I really could do with it was to find ratios. Handheld calculators would have been more fun, but they hadn't been invented yet. The commission itself had nothing but adding machines to work with, although we did finally acquire a new Monroe calculator that could do a few tricks, being blessed with something mysteriously described as a "memory."

While the testimony in rate cases was all about figures, we got "demonstrative" evidence in other cases, and some of it was memorable. I remember, in a complaint case about poor water service, the fruit jar of water that turned black when shaken. In another case one of the railroad brotherhoods complained that two railroad tracks were too close together. We had no trouble agreeing with the complainants after we were shown a trainman's jacket with the back torn to shreds. One of the most entertaining pieces of evidence was introduced during a war waged by the commission's staff on a dozen or more little telephone companies in the hinterlands. Some telephone lines to outlying customers were strung on tree limbs and fence posts. The switchboards dated back to the days of the old song "Hello, Central. Give me Heaven." "Central" in at least one of our companies was a housewife with a little oaken switchboard on the kitchen wall and more than enough to do besides switching calls. A classic snapshot told the story: a toddler was batting the headphones hanging free from the switchboard above his playpen. But people loved those phone companies. Screams rose when we put them out of business and parceled out the territories to General Telephone and Ohio Bell.

I marvel at the revolution in information technology since the early 1960s. Back then, for example, we were learning about such things as TASI, time assignment speech interpolation, a new Bell System sampling technique for increasing the message capacity of telephone lines. Today we read about conserving bandwidth by breaking phone messages into pieces and reassembling them at the far end. We never heard of bandwidth. Fashion had taken us only as far as Princess handsets, and technology hadn't taken us much farther. Fiber optics didn't exist. We couldn't have imagined today's ubiquitous cellular phones or any form of wireless telephony. Today, even more remarkably, we have gone from hand-cranked calculators to computers of incredible capacity. The Internet wasn't so much as a dream in our day, much less Internet telephoning—no e-mail, no instant messaging. I remember visiting Bell Labs in 1961, and nothing like what we know today was being predicted. The newest thing we saw was a red beam described as a ruby laser for which uses were being sought.

Most of our decisions are meaningless as precedents today in the new world of utility deregulation, but a couple may have some historical interest. One was to permit the New York Central to abandon passenger service between Cleveland, Columbus, and Cincinnati. The service was sacrosanct as long as Chief Justice Weygandt of the Ohio Supreme Court was taking the train from Cleveland to Columbus each week (and sleeping on the couch in his office). Then we permitted service to be reduced to a single, self-propelled car, a "Budd" car, and only when even the Budd car rolled along empty most of the time did we authorize abandonment. From time to time a grand proposal is made to restore passenger train service in Ohio, and the Cleveland-Columbus-Cincinnati connection is always central to the concept. It would make wonderful sense—if only people could be induced to use it.

I am frequently reminded of another historical decision when United Parcel Service makes deliveries in my neighborhood. UPS was a fairly small outfit when it applied in the early 1960s to the commission for authority to carry packages of certain small sizes and dimensions to a central point to be sorted and gathered by destination and then transshipped. This was a shocking idea, opposed by the trucking industry. Common carriers were narrowly regulated at that time, in both intrastate and interstate commerce, operating only over regular routes (between two given points) or over irregular routes (from and to a given point). "Breaking bulk" en route and transshipping were unthinkable. The proposal was even more violently opposed by Railway Express, which saw its unique advantage being threatened in that it already had the freedom to gather in packages from anywhere to any destination on railroad lines and then deliver them locally by truck. It took a very bold reading of Ohio's motor carrier laws to find authority for what UPS proposed. Our attorney examiner, Bill McGinnis, was able to reason his way persuasively past prohibitive precedents to recommend what he saw as a practical and defensible innovation. We accepted his recommendation and the decision was upheld by the Ohio Supreme Court on appeal.

From time to time, utilities hoped to educate us by taking us to see interesting facilities. I owe two of the scariest moments in my life to a couple of those tours. The first, arranged by The Cincinnati Gas and Electric Company—now Cinergy—was to see a gas storage reservoir in a limestone cave on the Kentucky side of the Ohio River across from Cincinnati. The ability to store the gas would permit it to be purchased at lower cost when demand was not at its peak. The cave wasn't a natural cave. It had been created first in bedrock with an auger. When a deep enough shaft had been opened, someone was dropped in "with a spoon," they said, to enlarge the hole. Then mining equipment was cut apart and sent down the shaft, welded back together at the bottom, and put to work. At last an immense chamber big enough to hold 7,500,000 gallons of propane gas was created. Our tour was to give us the opportunity to explore the chamber before it was filled.

After we lightly signed our lives away, we were dropped down the shaft, two at a time, in a tin can strung on a steel cable and let down from the boom of a crane parked beside the opening. The cable was threaded though an iron pipe, and we hung onto the pipe, facing each other, as the can de-

Riding the tin can down to the gas storage reservoir, 1961.

scended. The clangor was fearsome. We bonged and gebonged against the side walls all the way down. Worse still, when the tin can reached the end of the shaft it began to twirl around in the open space. Two men hung on to the length of cable below the can to steady us as we were lowered to the floor, but they weren't too helpful. When I was a little girl, we lowered a friend's cat, covered up in a basket, from the height of a second-story porch. It came out all fur and claws, and that is pretty much the way I came out of that can. Of course, what we saw was wondrous and never to be seen by human eyes again after the cavern was filled with gas. The white walls of limestone had a sooty band at the top like the crown molding of a Victorian parlor. It was soot laid down by Old Smoky, we were told, in its incarnation as a volcano.

The other scariest moment came on the top floor of Ohio Power's Philip

Sporn power plant, then under construction near Ravenswood, West Virginia. It never crossed my mind to be afraid as we rose to the top of the plant in a perfectly ordinary elevator—it was as if we were going to a penthouse—so when we got off the elevator I strolled casually across the floor toward what would someday be a wall. But there was no wall. I was looking out over empty space so far above the ground that cars and trucks below looked like toys. Somehow I managed to back up to the housing for the elevator, and I clung to it by my fingernails until someone finally pried me loose to go down again.

I never was good at power plants. Many years later, I had to step on someone's coat to be persuaded to get off the elevator at the top of Ohio Edison's Bruce Mansfield plant in Shippingport, Pennsylvania. The flat roof itself had a shallow wall around it, but the elevator door opened a few steps below the roof onto the usual power plant floor made of iron grillwork through which I could see everything below for twenty-six stories.

After Marty Galvin left and Ed Kenealy retired in 1961, the commission was more interesting but not as much fun. I was named chairman by Governor Mike DiSalle to succeed Ed, but the designation was not inevitable because the governor was appointing his own assistant, Rankin Gibson, to fill the vacancy, and he could have reasonably named him chairman. Rankin

FIRST WOMAN CHAIRMAN

Frances McGovern Gets Top PUCO Post At 34

Di Salle Picks Rate Law Foe

By ROBERT KOTZBAUER

The front page of the *Akron Beacon Journal*, December 29, 1961.

was superbly qualified to be chairman—indeed, to do almost anything. But justice prevailed. In other words, I got the appointment. There was a brief time when it seemed that Rankin nevertheless expected to run the commission, and single-handedly, but the three of us worked this out pleasantly. Before he left office, Mike appointed Rankin to the Ohio Supreme Court, a well-deserved promotion.

The biggest problem for me in 1961 was that I was not being confirmed by the Ohio Senate after I was appointed to a full term of six years. Neither were many other DiSalle appointees, because the Republicans had recaptured a majority in the Senate in 1960 and hoped to elect a Republican governor in 1962 with all his marvelous powers to make appointments to the Public Utilities Commission and other state agencies. I hung a sign on my door: "Unconfirmed Roomer."

Then came an unexpected turn of events. An unconfirmed member of the state Racing Commission challenged the right of the Senate to confirm appointments, and the Ohio Supreme Court, to everyone's astonishment, found the Senate had no power to do so, although it had been confirming routinely for generations. Hooray! I was home free, "confirmed" by the Supreme Court—or so I thought until a resolution was proposed in the Ohio House to put a constitutional amendment on the ballot that would not only "restore" the Senate's confirmation power, but also "reach back" to put all of us who thought we had escaped the Senate's clutches back in jeopardy.

The proposal was made in the Ohio House by Harold Oyster of Marietta, with whom I had served three terms. I thought he was a friend, but, by his lights, the potential for future patronage easily outweighed friendship. Luckily, Roger Cloud of Logan County, the Republican Speaker of the House with whom I had worked and even cosponsored legislation, wasn't so partisan. He asked Harold to withdraw the reach-back provision, and Harold, with feet dragging, finally did so. The voters gave the Senate confirmation power the following November without putting any of us unconfirmed roomers back in jeopardy.

One of the perquisites of being a commissioner was membership in the National Association of Railroad and Utility Commissioners, known as NARUC. As regulation of railroads faded away, the "RUC" of NARUC has since become "Regulatory Utility Commissions"—and properly so. Even in my day, there was so little regulation of railroads by state commissions that we used to be amused by a resolution demanding more boxcars, offered each year by a commissioner named Rasmussen from Minnesota, whose commission was uniquely a Railroad Commission. The NARUC annual meetings took me for the first time to New Orleans, San Francisco, and Atlantic City, regional meetings took me to the Greenbrier, and after Everett Krueger arranged for me to succeed him on the NARUC Executive Committee, I attended committee meetings in Washington many times and once, happily, in Jackson Hole, Wyoming.

I had one friend in Washington whom I had met in Los Angeles—Katie Louchheim, vice-chairman of the Democratic National Committee in 1960 and, after Kennedy's election, assistant secretary of state. She was a beautiful woman and a poet. She and her husband, an early member of the Securities and Exchange Commission staff, had known all the major figures of the New Deal, and she later wrote about them in *The Making of the New Deal.* Once when I was in Washington she asked if I would like to meet Lady Chesham from Tanganyika (who would not be intrigued?) and sent her car, a Rolls Royce, to pick me up for lunch. That was enough to bowl me over, but for good measure she called Jane Lausche, Senator Frank Lausche's wife, to join us, sure that I must know her since we were both from the same neighborhood, that is, Ohio. Jane Lausche, a charming person whom I had barely met, kindly treated me as an old friend. As for Lady Chesham, she turned out to be an Englishwoman, a widow who had lived in Tanganyika with her husband for many years. She had only recently been released from house arrest for working with Julius Nyerere for independence from Great Britain. Later, she was a member of the parliament of the independent Tanzania.

The regional Great Lakes Conferences of NARUC were annual delights, being that they always took place at the fabled Greenbrier Hotel. It didn't trouble anyone that the Greenbrier was in White Sulfur Springs, West Virginia, which is not one of our Great Lakes states. Indeed, Delaware, New Jersey, and Maryland also felt free to belong to our conference, as did Kentucky and even the Virgin Islands. The commissioners from the latter arrived one year hoping to persuade us to come to the Virgin Islands instead of the Greenbrier. They were unsuccessful but didn't seem to mind coming back to try again, year after year. The Greenbrier being somewhat expensive for travelers on state business, I asked a little nervously at the PUCO how it was justified. The answer was that we were on the American Plan, thus presumably immune to the blandishments of free meals offered by the utility people who came to the conference in great numbers. Fortunately for the pleasure of our stay, we were not immune to the blandishments of cocktail parties, wine at dinner, and free drinks in the Old White Club. In West Virginia, the sale of liquor by the drink was illegal, but the bartenders sold setups and brightened them from the proprietary bottles of the patrons. We sometimes adjourned to an after-hours joint at the end of the evening. There were two of them in the 1960s, also illegal, which took turns being open each month or, better said, took turns not being closed down by the sheriff.

All my enjoyment of the commission and pride in its work came to an end in January 1963 after James A. Rhodes beat Mike DiSalle for governor in the 1962 election. Two new commissioners, Carl Johnson and Warren Bettes, were appointed by the new governor. Carl, a mild-mannered lawyer from Westerville, became the new chairman, and the new majority appointed Sam Nicola as secretary. Nicola, I was told, had been cited more than once by our inspectors for unlawful operation of his local trucking business. I said I would sign his appointment if he assured me he had disposed of his interest in his trucking concern. He assured me he had done so. It soon turned out he had transferred it to his wife.

Carl had the premises swept for bugs and used to arrive each morning with a locked briefcase, apparently as suspicious off premises as on. The elevator was locked except for use by the commissioners. I was assumed to be involved in some kind of secret warfare. Carl said to me one day, "I give up. We've looked everywhere and can't find the budget. Will you kindly tell us where it is." I certainly hadn't hidden it away and didn't know where it was but suggested we look under *B* for "budget" in the secretary's filing cabinet. There it was. Another day, Carl told me he couldn't understand why we had never recognized the merits of a certain person on the staff. I said we had never discovered any merits. (In the end, neither did Carl.)

We stopped meeting as a commission, and orders were prepared for the other commissioners without so much as a copy being given me until they were about to be issued. Sam Nicola fired people wholesale on Friday afternoons at four o'clock for the sin of being Democrats or Independents, so no one on the staff dared talk to me until I persuaded Carl to assign someone to help me who was politically secure. One of the first to be fired was the head of the telephone section, Basil Boritski, who was nationally acclaimed for expertise in the arcane area of telephone rate case separations and had been at the PUCO for twenty-one years. Another was Bill Lindsay, who had recently earned his doctorate in utility economics and had just bought a house. Bill later held major positions at the Federal Energy Regulatory Commission in Washington. He never again bought a house. I protested. I exclaimed. Finally, I gave up any hope of being effective and resigned, as of July 1, 1963, with nearly four years still left in my term.

Strange to say, Carl and I later formed a wary alliance, partly because he ran into problems of his own in getting confirmed. I wrote to him with real sympathy of my days as an "unconfirmed roomer." He enjoyed that and put up his own sign. Some years later, when I was with Ohio Edison, I sat across from him at dinner one night at Congress Lake. Somehow an olive got away from me and disappeared where I could hardly retrieve it in polite company. I hoped no one had noticed, but when I looked up, Carl was beaming at me. We both laughed out loud and were good friends ever after.

Sixteen A New Run

Inevitably a successful politician aspires to higher office. Fred Harter reduced this to a formula which he imparted to me in my first term in the legislature: three terms and up. It was a formula he followed himself, running for the Senate after three terms in the Ohio House. I wasn't interested in the Senate, even supposing I wanted to run against my friends Fred Harter and Oliver Ocasek, who were the incumbents. Running for the U.S. Congress was one thing I could consider, however. Running for judge was another. I could see while I was in the legislature that I was gradually acquiring a beautiful resume for a judgeship. Not only was I a member and then chairman of the House Judiciary Committee, but the chairmanship automatically made me a member of the Ohio Judicial Council with members of the Ohio Supreme Court. The council almost never met, but being on it sounded great. I was on both the Akron and Ohio State Bar Association committees on judicial administration and legal reform. I wrote an article on the minor courts for the Ohio State University Law Journal. The trouble was that I had very little trial experience. Worse still, I never wanted to be a trial judge, and couldn't expect to skip up to the appellate level.

For me, appointment to the Ohio Public Utilities Commission had been the perfect answer. We were dealing with subjects that fascinated me, and, while we were undoubtedly judges in my day, presiding over hearings and basing conclusions on evidence produced under the usual rules, almost all the testimony consisted of interesting, often clashing, opinions of witnesses, qualified as "expert," on issues very unlike those in a court of law.

When I resigned from the PUCO, however, I was too beaten down to have any other aspirations. Besides, I had lost my anchor in Akron when my father died in 1961 and my sister and I sold the house on Vinita Avenue where I had lived my entire life. All I wanted was simply to anchor myself again. I never considered living anywhere but Akron—I even came home from Columbus to the Holiday Inn on West Market Street on weekends after the house was sold. When I moved back to Akron, I bought a house of my own on Woodside Drive in Akron, with wonderful oak trees and a deep ravine, and I gratefully returned to my former law office with John Quine. I also bought my dear Cherry, a Kerry blue terrier, who arrived by air freight from Bucks County, Pennsylvania. We worriedly sized each other up, with milk bones proffered and eaten as I drove her home from the airport. She checked out the house and then the yard, at length and inch by inch. When she came back in, I gave her a hug, and she gave me a kiss. Both of us now had a home and both of us intended to stay.

I had long had an interest in running for Congress, but I felt I had made a choice against it when I went to the PUCO. It seemed to me that it was a little late to reconsider when I came home. Except as a convention delegate, I hadn't been on the ballot for five years. That's a long time to be out of touch. Only think! I hadn't been to a picnic, a card party, a rally, a covered-dish supper, a spaghetti dinner, or a fish fry in all those years. I didn't even know all the ward leaders anymore, or the newer officeholders.

The biggest reason of all, however, for not running for Congress was Bill Ayres, who was virtually unbeatable. I had watched him win easily ever since he was first elected in 1950.

William H. Ayres, congressman from the Fourteenth District of Ohio, was a phenomenon—a Republican in Democratic territory who had already been elected to Congress seven times before I came home and was going to be elected three more times after that, serving, all told, from 1951 to 1971. Clyde Mann told me that Ayres was "discovered" in 1950 by Ray Bliss, then the chairman of the Summit County Republican Party. Bliss, the story goes, was looking for someone who could beat Walter Huber, the well-entrenched Democratic congressman, when he saw ads in the *Akron Beacon Journal* for Ayres's heating company. I remember the ads. They featured a photograph of Ayres looking smart and sassy, with slicked-down hair and a big smile. Ayres had no political affiliation at the time, had maybe never even voted, but Ray Bliss had a good eye for talent. Ayres turned out to be a natural in politics—easy to meet and a wow with the ladies of the Eighth Ward Women's Republican Club. Upon Ray Bliss's urging, he ran for Congress against Huber in 1950, and he won.

How he won, however, raised a legal question. Although Lorain County was a Democratic stronghold in the four-county Fourteenth Congressional District in 1950, Ayres got a surprisingly big vote in that county. Investigation revealed that Ayres's name was listed first on all the ballots, not rotated approximately precinct by precinct with Huber's name, as required by law. It was assumed this had given Ayres an unearned advantage, and Huber promptly sued to overturn the outcome. But he lost the case, probably because failure to rotate names didn't confuse anyone or deprive anyone of a choice. All the suit did was mark Huber as a poor loser—politically a kiss of death. When Huber ran against Ayres again in 1952, he lost in part because of his lawsuit.

By 1952, however, Bill Ayres had more than that lawsuit to help him. He had recruited a first-rate staff, eager to serve constituents, and he was friendly enough to the interests of the labor unions to keep Democrats off balance. He also was a great champion of veterans, and there were lots of them in both parties in the 1950s. But Democrats don't give up easily, at least not in territory they believe belongs to them.

Taking on Ayres in 1954 was John L. Smith from Barberton, who spoke in rolling periods like a senator and, although he was still a young man,

John Smith

looked like a senator too, with a big head of white hair like the mane of the durable John Bricker, U.S. senator from Ohio, former governor, and 1944 Republican nominee for vice president, once described by Arthur M. Schlesinger Jr. as "central casting's idea of a senator." The only one who could overshadow John was his mother, Elizabeth Smith, an imposing matron, long a force in the Democratic Party in Barberton, to whom he paid tribute at every opportunity. He also had a wife, Betty, whom everyone liked, although we all guessed it would have been dangerous for him to pay tribute to her when his mother was present. Ayres defeated John, despite John's fair prospects.

In many ways, it was too bad John lost. He had considerable ability and was eager for an opportunity to show what he could do. Two years later, in 1956, he ran successfully for state representative, but it was a step below his ambition, and he seemed to lose his spirit. He did a good job, and I enjoyed serving with him, but we sometimes had to cover for him when people from home came to see us in the legislature. "He must be here somewhere because his hat is on his desk," we would say. But his hat was there more often than he was. He was running for reelection in 1958 when he died suddenly. His wife then ran for his seat and won. Betty was at least as bright as John, and she had held a major civil service position in Washington before she and John were married. I particularly liked her, and we became good friends. Sadly, however, one term was all she could take, lonely and away from her two young sons most of the week for the many weeks the legislature was in session.

Next to run against Ayres was my old friend Bernie Rosen, who had been the campaign manager when I got my start in politics at the old Backstage Bar headquarters. Bernie, a witty, well-liked lawyer, was often sought after to manage campaigns, and he managed a good many of them for the party and for individual candidates, but it was harder to manage his own campaign. In 1956, President Eisenhower was running for reelection, and he was not only popular but he also had coattails, which few presidential candidates have had since then. The coattails gave Ayres an extra margin when he won his fourth term. Mike DiSalle, who would later make such a difference in my life when he appointed me to the PUCO, lost too on his first run for governor against C. William O'Neill that year.

I have two pictures of Bernie and me from Bernie's campaign for Congress in 1956 and my campaign for reelection as state representative. I don't know which I treasure more. It should be the first, a picture of the two of us with Eleanor Roosevelt. But I think I favor the second. It was in the *Akron Beacon Journal*. Bernie and I are sitting together. Bernie is pulling up his pants leg to show me the bite he got from a dog who thought poorly of door-to-door campaigners, and I am laughing.

The picture with Eleanor Roosevelt was taken at The University of Akron when she came there to speak. She had said she'd like to visit with "a young person" before she spoke. I was thrilled to be chosen and went to her room at the Mayflower an hour before she was due to leave for the university. It was the longest hour of my life. She turned out to be very deaf, and that was just as well, because I turned out to be nearly speechless, overwhelmed

Bernie Rosen showing me the dog bite he received while campaigning, 1956.

Meeting with
Eleanor Roosevelt
and Bernie
Rosen, 1956.

with trying to find something weighty to say. My lasting impression was simply of her kind smile and her great height when she stood up to go.

I remember better the ride to the university. Mrs. Roosevelt didn't want a police escort, and she even wanted to sit in the front seat with the driver, like any ordinary passenger. You can guess what that set off when we stopped at the traffic light at Broadway and Center Streets and a car with a big family of children pulled up beside us. The father glanced over. First, his eyes nearly popped out of his head. Then the car practically bulged with the family's reaction. Mrs. Roosevelt was known for her travels and for turning up almost anywhere, but nothing had prepared an Akron family to see her smile and nod to them from the next car.

Half the fun of being in politics came from treats like that one. I had another in 1956 when I went to Washington for a meeting of women legislators. There weren't many of us in those days, and most came from New England where great numbers of towns had representatives. Someone with connections arranged for us to meet Mamie Eisenhower in the White

House. It was on June 7, 1956, at 10:15 A.M. I know because I still have the White House pass. Mrs. Eisenhower was not only vivacious, but she was also surprisingly girlish in a swing skirt that she enjoyed swishing around. She took us to a basement room where the china of various presidencies was displayed. Gathering it had been one of her own projects, clearly one she liked, and she gave us the history of each setting.

Something else happened in 1956—important to no one else, I am sure, but treasured as a great triumph by me. It happened in October of 1956 at Kent State University at a forum on foreign policy. David Dennison from Warren, Ohio, the Republican candidate for Congress in the Eleventh Congressional District, was asked to speak, but his Democratic opponent wasn't campaigning at all, so I was asked to speak for Democratic positions. Someone laid a trap for me in the question-and-answer period. Did I agree with a certain strong pronouncement on foreign policy by the Democratic state chairman of New Jersey? I said I did—in fact, I could think of no better authority on the subject than the Democratic chairman, he being George F. Kennan, an architect of the Marshall Plan and better known as Mr. X, the author of a celebrated article in *Foreign Affairs* advocating "containment" of communism.

This gave me confidence that I could be "congressional." I also could hardly fail to notice in 1956 that I had far more votes in my race than Ayres had in his. The races were not really comparable, because in 1956 candidates for state representative from Summit County were still running at large and five were to be chosen. That meant I could theoretically be someone's fifth choice and still get a vote. But the total vote I got was high enough to make me thoughtful. I received 122,145 votes in coming in first for the legislature. (John Smith was second of five with 108,574.) Ayres's total was only 108,387 votes in Summit and Medina Counties combined. What if I ran for Congress? The thought came and went, came and went over the next several years, but I put the thought behind me when I went to the Public Utilities Commission.

In any event, in 1958 and 1960 others were interested, and there were spirited contests in the Democratic primaries in both years for the opportunity to run against Ayres. Two of the candidates ran both times. One was George Mark, the man who had hired trumpeters for a tribute at one of the Jefferson-Jackson Day dinners. The other was John Mihaly, who had rushed forward to take the tribute for himself with his sign, as I described in chapter 5. The winner in 1958, however, was neither of them. It was Jack B. Arnold, a likable fellow whose father, Kurt Arnold, was a well-known jeweler in East Akron but who was virtually unknown himself. It was a good year for a Democrat to run, but not someone brand new to the ballot. Not even the huge Democratic vote was enough to carry Arnold in the general election in 1958 when labor turned out in force to vote no on the right-to-work proposal. Ayres won with nearly 60 percent of the vote, and in 1960 he won with an even higher percentage when John Mihaly was the nominee. It wasn't until 1962 that Oliver Ocasek, safely running in the middle of his first four-year term as state senator, gave Ayres a real run for his money. But Oliver lost too.

Who would run in 1964? Somewhat to my surprise, I was asked to do so. If I remember right, the approach came from Ed Erickson, by then mayor of Akron, and Don Luffman, his political ally and friend. I see them sitting in my living room on Woodside Drive and telling me that a poll indicated I had a better chance of winning against Ayres than Oliver Ocasek or Ed himself. But this is an unreliable memory. I also cannot say what gave me the idea then or later that I was merely expected to hold a place for Ed to run himself the next time.

In the end, vanity, the principal support of most candidates, persuaded me to run. Everyone is really good at something, and I had decided when I was in the legislature that legislating was the one thing I was really good at. Of course, I also had some ideas about issues, but it was the process of legislating more than any issues that appealed to me.

It is hard to imagine that vanity supported John Mihaly's decision to run, too. The snaggletoothed "Mayor of Goosetown" was a perennial loser. Maybe he thought his campaigns for Congress would bring him business as a public accountant. Maybe he just hoped fate would put him in office. If John got through the primary and Ayres thereupon died or withdrew too late to be replaced by the Republican Party before the general election, John would be congressman by default. Whatever may have been his virtues, his appearance and manners appalled anyone picturing him as Akron's emissary in Washington. When John was, in fact, the Democratic nominee in 1960, the prayers for Ayres's good health came from members of both parties.

At first, Mihaly's running for Congress in the Democratic primary in 1964 was of no great concern to me. I was pretty sure I would win. But early in the spring, I got a call from Katie Louchheim in Washington. Katie was as well connected in the Johnson administration as she had been in the Kennedy administration when she first became assistant secretary of state. Johnson, after succeeding to the presidency upon the tragic death of John Kennedy in 1963, was gearing up to run for president on his own account, and to that end he was appointing many women to major positions in the government.

That's what occasioned Katie's call. Would I be interested in serving on the Securities and Exchange Commission, she asked me. Would I? That was almost beyond dreams. To me, appointment to the SEC was the most prestigious in all of Washington. Without ever thinking of being a member, I had been interested in the SEC for years. In fact, in my college days at The University of Akron, where I majored in economics, my senior thesis was on the reasons for creating the SEC. The fact that I wasn't qualified didn't bother me.

The appointment was not Katie's to give, of course, but she had great influence, especially on women's appointments, because of her days as vice-chairman of the Democratic National Committee, which, politically speaking, meant she represented the women in the party. She also had ties to the

SEC herself since its creation. Her husband had been a distinguished member of the SEC staff—one of the first brought in when the commission was created in 1933. Katie gave me to believe that she was also sounding me out for Don Cook, the president of American Electric Power and a former member of the SEC. That was a surprise to me. I had met Cook when I was at the Public Utilities Commission, but I doubted I had endeared myself to him in any way.

For a few wild moments, new house, Akron, Congress, and everything else suddenly seemed unimportant. In less than an hour, however, I called Katie back, unhappy and disposed to slaughter John Mihaly. I realized I couldn't pursue the appointment because, if it came through, John would be left unopposed to run against Ayres. We would be back to praying for Ayres's good health.

Less than three weeks later, when the great opportunity had passed, John Mihaly unexpectedly died. It was I who was now unopposed to run against Ayres. My feet were still dragging a little because of my lost opportunity, but I soon brightened up. The campaign was beginning to look exciting, if not yet very promising. Another Democratic National Convention was coming along, and I was again a delegate. I also could look forward to a White House conference for new Democratic candidates for Congress. I could be reasonably sure the underlying Democratic vote in the Fourteenth District would help bring in some money from elsewhere for the campaign. And, it was hinted, some major figure might come in to help the cause along.

Seventeen The 1964 Campaign

Memories are not only selective. They have a way of sorting themselves out in favorite order. There were quite a few remarkable events when I ran for Congress in 1964, including the tea for Lady Bird Johnson, Johnson's big day in Akron, Franklin Roosevelt Jr.'s coming in to campaign for me, the Democratic National Convention, and a visit to the White House. Of all those memorable events and several others, the one that always comes out on top is of Hubert Humphrey's Labor Day visit to Barberton on September 2, 1964. Who would have thought that Barberton's parade, starting at the west end of Wooster Road and ending at the old bathhouse on Lake Anna, was the second biggest celebration of Labor Day in the whole country? Only Detroit drew a bigger crowd. In Barberton, some seventy thousand people were expected, far more than Barberton's entire population. It was well worth a campaign visit from Humphrey, running for vice president in Johnson's triumphal year.

I was just a tagalong, but Humphrey generously made sure I got all the good a congressional candidate could from the presidential campaign. When his day began in Akron, reporters and photographers crowded around him at the Sheraton Mayflower Hotel. Humphrey not only pulled me in beside him, but he also pinned my arm to his side because he saw I was a little hesitant to push into his show. He also insisted that I ride with him and Senator Stephen M. Young out to Barberton and in the parade. That I was hoping for. I was dressed like a homecoming queen, white gloves and all, for the ride of a lifetime, sitting on top of the back seat of a four-door convertible.

The day was clear and sunny, a perfect day for flags, crowds, and parades. But, of course, it was also a great day for picnics and other family diversions, and in Akron, where no one knew Humphrey's route, or even when or if he would pass, no one, absolutely no one, was to be seen on Akron's Wooster Avenue and then East Avenue on the way to Barberton. A dog passed in front of us, and we assured Humphrey that it was a Democrat, but Humphrey was starting to worry about the turnout.

"It's all right," I told him. "No one is expecting you in Akron. Wait until we get to Barberton." But when we came into Barberton on Wooster Road North, with the city limits sign in plain view, there still was no crowd—no traffic whatsoever, not even anyone on a front porch. The stillness suggested a tragedy had occurred. Things were no better when we turned up Hopocan Avenue to take a back way to the far end of town where the parade was to begin on Wooster Road West at about 21st Street. The stillness was beginning to bother Steve Young by then, and even me. No dog or cat, no kids, no bicycles. Not even a breeze to lift the leaves on the trees. The cars we passed were parked and empty. "They're all waiting for you along the route," I said, but I was losing my conviction. Then, finally, we heard a glorious blast of music from the Barberton Magics All Brass Band not more than a couple of blocks away, and we came in through a jam-packed side street to where the parade was waiting for its star player. We let out our breaths together in a long, relieved gasp.

"Hubert, Hubert," people began to call, and Hubert came alive, waving happily to everyone, and murmuring "Hello, there! Hello, there! Hello there!" into the noise of the crowd for the whole length of the parade. Secret Service men, unmistakable "suits," walked warily beside and behind us.

I was happy to hear an occasional call of "Fran, Fran" too, and even more so to see one of my big blue, green, and white campaign signs pushed up above the crowd on a long pole. At the bottom of the pole was David Thompson, my fourteen-year-old next-door neighbor on Woodside Drive, and one of his friends. It was quite a surprise. I had no idea David was going to do this. It was even more of a surprise when I saw the same sign rising above the crowd at intervals along the route. David and his friend, getting redder and hotter at each stop, were running behind the crowds to greet us again. "You have a good many supporters," Humphrey said to me when the sign went up ahead of us for the third or fourth time. "Well, yes and no," I

Campaigning with Vice President Hubert Humphrey and Senator Stephen M. Young in Barberton Labor Day parade, 1964.

said. "Look close. It's the same kids every time." That struck Humphrey as funny. After that, he waved especially and specifically to the boys, and, of course, they loved it, and it gave them the energy for another long run ahead.

Humphrey didn't need to prepare a speech for his arrival at Lake Anna. He already had one. He knew it by heart, and the crowd knew it too. He had given the speech first at the Democratic National Convention a couple of weeks earlier when he accepted the nomination to run for vice president with Lyndon Johnson. We all counted on him to say again what Democrats were for and Barry Goldwater was against, and we were eager to help him lay it out.

Senator Goldwater had been doing a good job of defeating himself ever since he was nominated for president by the Republican National Convention in San Francisco in mid-July. He had spoken so strongly about meeting force with force that the famous words of his acceptance speech, "Extremism in the defense of liberty is no vice," although arguably spoken in a narrower context, led voters to fear he would resort to atomic warfare. He was against ratifying the Nuclear Test Ban Treaty. He had voted against the Civil Rights Act of 1964. He was against the War on Poverty, Medicare, and other popular measures, and wanted to make Social Security voluntary. He was a sitting duck. After some kind words for Steve Young and me, Humphrey launched the speech everyone was waiting for. (I can't remember the words so I have to paraphrase the lead-ins to Humphrey's unforgettable refrain.)

"Democrats believe that poverty is unacceptable and are working to end it," Humphrey said. "But *not* Senator Goldwater!" The audience heard its cue. "Democrats favor the preservation and strengthening of Social Security." he continued. "But . . ." "*Not* Senator Goldwater!" the crowd chorused with him. "Democrats favor the provision of medical care for the elderly," he said. The crowd finished the thought for him: "But *not* Senator Goldwater!" After the pump was primed a third time, there was no need for Humphrey to sing out at all. He had only to conduct the refrain with his hands. The crowd shouted it joyfully, in full voice.

Hubert Humphrey had been the obvious choice for vice president at the Democratic National Convention in August, but, because his own nomination for president was a foregone conclusion, Johnson evidently thought the delegates would be bored if he announced his choice before the last minute. He went through the motions of considering other candidates, including Senator Ribicoff of Connecticut, Robert Wagner, the mayor of New York, and Eugene McCarthy, Humphrey's fellow senator from Minnesota. I was a delegate to the convention, and I remember he called Humphrey to Washington to be interviewed as if he couldn't make up his mind among applicants. But I don't think any of us were fooled. The only other candidate besides Humphrey who would have been as popular was Bobby Kennedy, and late in June, Johnson said he had decided not to choose anyone for vice president who was in his cabinet or met with it. That, of course, settled it for Kennedy, who was attorney general. It also eliminated Orville Freeman, secretary of agriculture; Adlai Stevenson, by then delegate to the United Nations; Robert McNamara, secretary of defense; and some other marginal contenders.

Kennedy said at the time he was sorry he took so many good men with him. He spoke even more plainly a couple of weeks later at a briefing session I went to in Washington for Democrats running for Congress. "I really envy you," he said. "All of you can be considered for the vice presidency." We laughed ruefully in sympathy.

I for one wasn't bored for a minute at the 1964 convention in Atlantic City. The city was a little seedy. The boardwalk was end-to-end honky-tonk. But I loved finding myself on the Monopoly gameboard and smiled every time I saw street names like Ventnor, Marvin Gardens, New York, and St. James, and postcards of Monopoly's jail inscribed "Just Visiting." One important drama I missed. A Freedom Party formed by blacks, who were denied the vote in Mississippi, sought recognition for its delegates. The credentials committee came up with a rule requiring voting for delegates to future conventions to be open to all. But that left the issue mostly unresolved in 1964, and the rejected delegates marched into the convention. On our side of the hall, we weren't aware of any disturbance until we read about it later.

A memorable event was the sad reception for Jacqueline Kennedy. It was held in a small room, almost a hallway, with a door at each end. We went through in single file, giving our condolences, one by one. Outside, Pierre Salinger, Kennedy's press secretary and now senator from California, offered two of us a ride back to our hotel in a limousine waiting for him, and, of course, we accepted.

One big excitement for me was being in the honor guard that accompanied the convention's keynote speaker, John O. Pastore, congressman from Rhode Island, to the dais. No doubt I was given the opportunity because I was running for Congress and could use the publicity back home, but I was too unpracticed in making news to capitalize on it, and, seated behind Pastore, I didn't even hear his speech.

Later, however, I did hear Robert Kennedy's tribute to his brother. For what seemed like forever before he could begin, we simply stood and applauded. I have never forgotten the sound of that long, sustained applause, voiceless and profound. Bobby tried to start speaking several times, only to be met with a new surge of emotion. When he finally was able to speak, the silence in which he was heard was another tribute. Half a lifetime later, I am in tears again, recalling the words he quoted from *Romeo and Juliet.*

> *(A)nd, when he shall die,*
> *Take him and cut him out in little stars,*
> *And he will make the face of heaven so fine*
> *That all the world will be in love with night*
> *And pay no worship to the garish sun.*

It was, however, stars of a different kind that I took home with me. During the ovation for Johnson's nomination, dazzling showers of red, silver, and blue foil stars were loosed on the crowd, the kind we got on good papers at school—Dennison stars with glue on the back. I was standing on my chair in stocking feet with my high-heeled red leather shoes on the floor in front of me. Quite a few stars ended up glued to the inner soles.

Back home, I was learning that times had changed since I ran for the legislature for the last time in 1958. First, I missed the little ward club meetings and suppers that sprang up early to give candidates some exposure. Apparently, they were no longer part of the political scene. Then, when I went down to the county engineer's office to get a new map of the picnic grounds, I couldn't find anyone who knew where they were, and when I went on Sundays to the old sites I remembered, I found that the "picnic circuit" was gone. There were now so few picnics that it had become necessary to know specifically who was having a picnic and where and when. The biggest shock came when I couldn't find the West Virginia Society's annual picnic. I remember it had been at Summit Beach Park in 1958, and Jennings Randolph of West Virginia, running for his first term in the U.S. Senate, was the speaker. By 1964, the society, one of Akron's most durable institutions, was dormant or dead, and Summit Beach had been closed for years.

I was also learning that running for Congress is different from running for the state legislature. For one thing, the campaign had to be better organized. John Quine had always let me use his name on ads as chairman of my campaigns, and I was proud to be associated with him, but I made all the few decisions that were necessary. That was all right with John. He wasn't all that interested in politics. (No one knew then that his wife, Jane, *was* interested and would later become the highly successful Democratic county chairman. In my day, she was busy enough raising a big family.)

Ralph Turner, the popular president of Akron City Council, was chairman of my campaign when I ran for Congress. He was a particularly good choice. A rubber worker with a soft Carolina accent who lived in Goodyear Heights, he compensated for my weakness as a West Hill candidate. I suspect he also had more common sense than I did, but he loyally supported me even when I was "wrong" by his lights. Best of all from my personal standpoint, he was married to Catherine Turner, the Democratic Party chairwoman. She had brought me up in politics. "Listen to me. I'm your mother," she used to say when she thought I was getting out of line, and I never minded a scolding because, having been born in Scotland, she spoke with a delightful burr. We also got Marvin Shapiro, now a highly regarded judge of the Akron Municipal Court but then a new young lawyer just starting out, to manage the day-to-day campaign activities on a part-time basis.

One reason why being organized was so important was that there were all these volunteers stepping forward to help. I was used to good will, but I had always campaigned pretty much on my own. This was different. People were interested in issues and success for the party, not just in me, and they wanted something useful to do. Campaigning was also an entertainment, and we wanted supporters to enjoy themselves. There was literature to address, signs to put up, meetings to cover, phones to answer, issues to research, strategy to think out, ads to be conceived, polls to take, and, in this campaign, some unusual tasks to be done.

A task I gave up very reluctantly was writing some of my speeches. We subscribed to *Congressional Quarterly,* which gave us material on the issues we were interested in, but it requires an unusual talent for one person to write for someone else. The late Maurie Reishtein was one who could do that. The other was John Seiberling, who ended up being a superb congressman himself after he was elected in 1970. John wrote a speech for me on world peace with rhythm or phrasing so like mine that, if it hadn't been so good, I would have thought I wrote it myself.

Another unusual task was to prepare a reception for Lady Bird Johnson, who was going to begin an early campaign on her own for the president. Her first stop was to be Akron. The purpose, of course, was to help her husband, but it was also to help me. Our committee easily decided to have a tea in the ballroom of the Sheraton Mayflower Hotel, the only place big enough and splendid enough to receive her. I am slightly embarrassed to report that we spent more time trying to think how to keep my name up front. At length,

Receiving line at the 1964 tea for Lady Bird Johnson, Mayflower Ballroom. *L to R:* Mrs. Leo Dugan, Beatrice Warwick, Lady Bird, me, Mrs. Anthony Celebrezze, Mrs. Jane Lausche, Mrs. Steve Young, Mary Barbuto, Catherine Turner.

someone came up with words we thought had a lovely, gracious tone while still giving me top billing:

Frances McGovern
and her guests
Welcome Mrs. Johnson

The words went up on a huge sign on the stage behind the receiving line.

Flags and bunting would be too ordinary for decorations. No problem there. A great idea came from Gladys Skorman. Her husband Albert and his brother had the Miracle Mart on State Road in Cuyahoga Falls with every kind of merchandise, including big wire trash burners. Gladys and other volunteers spray-painted them and hung them like giant bird cages, full of flowers. The event was going to be covered by national television, and that would require miles of cable. Incredibly, we also had a volunteer recently retired from the navy, Bob Lebo, who knew how to do everything. He provided a professional liaison with the network people and supervised the entire electrical installation.

The only hitch in our planning came when the local musicians' union protested the plan to have the Garfield High School band play for Mrs. Johnson's arrival at the Akron Municipal Airport the afternoon before the tea. There was an enthusiastic crowd to greet her at the airport but no music. In a short while, however, Elizabeth Carpenter, Lady Bird's press secretary, was going to show us how to turn a rebuff from the musicians' union to advantage.

Eighteen **Visitors**

Lady Bird Johnson had a mild, sweet way about her and sometimes an abstracted manner as if she was not aware of being the focus of attention. In that regard, I couldn't help thinking she was very unlike Rose Kennedy, who seemed to think all eyes were on her even when they weren't. In fact, it was possible to forget Mrs. Johnson briefly when Elizabeth Carpenter, her press secretary, was with her. Liz Carpenter was a Texan more like Lyndon than Lady Bird, expansive and people-centered. Plump and blue-haired, she almost exploded with energy when she had an idea, and she had lots of ideas.

She seemed to be satisfied with our plans for the tea the next afternoon when we went over them after she and Mrs. Johnson were settled at the hotel. But, she asked, what were we going to do *before* then? We told her some of the local officeholders such as Councilmen Ralph Turner, Ed Davis, Victor Herbert, and Jim Winter were coming in, but that was about it. I said we had been planning to have Mrs. Johnson tour Opportunity Park, an urban renewal project in the neighborhood around The B. F. Goodrich Company that was scheduled for clearance and redevelopment with federal funding. But the Secret Service, who had been out here for several days, had nixed the tour as too dangerous. Her eyes lit up. Was that the joy of battle I saw in them? I got the impression that, in Liz Carpenter's opinion, if plans were left to the Secret Service, there wouldn't be any campaign at all. New plans for Opportunity Park immediately began to take shape and, if Goodrich was just down the street, as close as we said, why, no bus would be necessary. We would all walk there from the hotel. The Secret Service men could walk with us, if they wished.

And, she asked, what was this she heard about the musicians' union preventing the Garfield High School Band from playing at the airport? Couldn't Lady Bird visit the school to make amends? "You won't believe this," I told them. "Harland Horton, the principal of Garfield High, just happens to be eating dinner downstairs at the Merry Man's Tavern. I saw him going in when we arrived." "Go and get him," Liz said. That wasn't hard. I flew downstairs. He was already finishing dinner and was delighted to come upstairs with me. In no time, we were scheduled to come out to the high school early the next morning. The band wouldn't play—no point in stirring up the musicians again—and we wouldn't go inside, but the students would all come out, and Mrs. Johnson would visit with them and shake hands.

The remarkable Mrs. Carpenter wasn't done yet. Next, she got in touch with Harvey Firestone Jr., which was more than we ever would have tried, even living here in Akron. Harvey Firestone had recently followed Henry Ford II's lead in endorsing Johnson. It took Liz Carpenter only one phone call to arrange for all the employees of the Firestone plants on South Main Street—we are talking about thousands of people—to be invited outside to meet Mrs. Johnson the next morning. Harvey himself would be at the front of the crowd. Jane Lausche, Senator Frank Lausche's wife, Steve Young's wife, and I would all go along. Our simple plans for the tea had turned into a royal progress. I had learned at Liz Carpenter's knee, so to speak, that in politics, news doesn't just happen. It gets made.

The big day, Friday, September 18, 1964, turned out to be rainy—not pouring but misty—and we didn't have any umbrellas. Someone reported that the tobacco shop in the hotel lobby had throwaway plastic raincoats, so I bought all they had—five of them. We were on such a tight budget, or at least I was personally, that I still remember that those raincoats cost fifty cents apiece. We wore them at Garfield, and the day never did brighten up, but it did get drier, and by the time we got to Firestone, we didn't need them any more. What we needed there was room to move! The crowd packed in so tight around us that the Secret Service men were having fits, and no wonder. If Lady Bird had been stabbed, she couldn't even have fallen over.

The crowd was much thinner in Opportunity Park. The Secret Service hadn't been able to head off the tour, but they had insisted there be no general announcement that Lady Bird was coming, so she was greeted by officialdom from Goodrich with charts and drawings—fair enough since

Lady Bird's 1964 visit to Firestone. *L to R:* Harvey S. Firestone, Sr. (back to camera), Lady Bird, me, Mrs. Steve Young.

Goodrich had advanced money to lay the foundation for urban renewal of the area. Nevertheless, a respectable crowd of children, dogs, and house-wives followed us through the neighborhood, alerted when camera trucks, reporters, and photographers began to take up positions. The neighbors made a better story than the charts for the evening news. A big American flag hanging from the window of one house made a perfect backdrop for one scene. For another, a woman stood on a porch with tears in her eyes, wringing her hands on her apron. When she saw the woman, Lady Bird went halfway up the porch steps to meet her, and every camera followed her. I heard later that the woman on the porch was married to Fire Chief Frank Vernotzy's brother.

Walking through the Opportunity Park area, I wasn't sure it was "blighted," but that was a condition of federal funding for renewal. The houses were old, the paint was sooty, the shops were certainly not showy, and ferns drooped in a few shop windows. Perhaps because I've lived all my life in Akron, the area nonetheless seemed alive and vital to me. A few years before, Hobart Schaefer, the Goodrich rubber worker who used to ride to Columbus with me, had taken me into each pool hall, lunchroom, cigar store, and storefront office on the stretch of Main Street across from Goodrich to meet friends of his, most of whom he knew by name. That was all cleared away for a glass office building for Goodrich that Goodrich deserted only a few years later. I had also visited Leo Dugan, president of the Summit-Medina Labor Council, at the council's office in an old house a short distance up the street. Although St. Mary's at Thornton Street always looked clean and well maintained, and it is still there, I did realize there was blight by some definition: I remember going one night to speak at a church on Bartges Street that was almost totally dark except for light welling up from a trap door with a staircase to a basement where the meeting was being held. The church itself was condemned for occupancy, but there was a pianist playing marvelously in blue notes and broken chords, and there was plenty of spirit. Channelwood Village and the handsome park beside the canal took the place of the houses and stores that used to be there. I know, I know. We can't live in the past. Yet, when the neighborhood was destroyed, and the people who lived there—black, white, and mostly old—were swept away to their children's homes or to Cape Cods a couple of miles away, I believe some part of Akron's soul died.

After the events of the morning, our tea—a woman's affair—was an anticlimax but crowded with well-wishers. A few of them clutched grandchildren they had brought for a glimpse of a real First Lady. One was Lillian Ryan who remembers her five-year-old grandchild couldn't get over having Lady Bird shake her hand and call her by her name, Margaret, even though her name tag was on upside down. Refreshments were being served in the adjacent small ballroom, but it was hard to get anyone to move away. Mrs. Lausche and Mrs. Young were with Mrs. Johnson and me in the receiving line in front of the stage, as was the wife of Anthony J. Celebrezze of Cleveland, who was then secretary of Health, Education and Welfare and later a judge of the U.S. Sixth Circuit Court of Appeals. Also in the line were Catherine Turner, Mary Barbuto, Leo Dugan's wife, and Beatrice Warwick of the United Rubber Workers. Conspicuous among those coming through the line were the "McGovern Girls," a lively bunch of North Hill teenagers dressed in red jackets and red straw hats who had skipped school for the occasion. I was worn out by then, but Mrs. Johnson was still fresh and shook hands with each person as if each were important.

There was no topping this as a campaign event, but there were still more visitors to come to Akron, partly because a Democratic Congressional Campaign Committee had marked this district as one that could be won. That action was also (a little belatedly) bringing in showers of money from afar, including, to my amazement, a big check from the International Ladies Garment Workers, which had never so much as basted a seam in Akron's Fourteenth Congressional District. The deadline for reserving television coverage, however, with cash up front, had long since passed, and we were hard put to spend the late money effectively.

Where was Bill Ayres when all these events were going on? He had been seen already that fall on the edge of our crowds with a steady smile despite rebuffs. But his particular interest was in sharing visitors, and his talent for attaching himself to any source of publicity was as well known in Washington as it was in Akron, especially after he rode a tricycle, intended for Caroline Kennedy, down the Capitol steps.

When Franklin D. Roosevelt Jr. flew in for a fund-raising luncheon for me, several of us met his plane at the Cleveland Airport. We watched as seemingly all of the passengers came off the plane, but not Roosevelt. Then, after a long pause, came—Ayres! He saw us waiting but stationed himself at the bottom of the steps. We waited again. Finally, there was Roosevelt in the doorway, with his father's famous smile. He came down the steps, giving Ayres only a nod on the way. "What happened?" we asked. Roosevelt said he saw Ayres get on the plane in Washington so he waited in Cleveland until Ayres got off, but then he saw him standing at the bottom of the steps. "I should have known I couldn't outlast him," Roosevelt said. "I'm the reason he was on the plane." Bill began to come our way, but we had a small plane ready to take us to Akron, and we closed in around Roosevelt, big and tall though he was, and hustled him across the tarmac out of Bill's reach.

Sargent Shriver, director of the Peace Corps and John F. Kennedy's brother-in-law (probably better known today as Maria Shriver's father), came to Akron to speak to an Akron Bar Association luncheon at the Mayflower. I wasn't above having my own picture taken with him, but I was a member of the bar and had paid for my ticket to the luncheon, so I figured that gave me the moral high ground to keep Shriver out of Ayres's clutches. Shriver delightedly agreed to foil any approach. Ayres, accompanied by a photographer, almost nailed him at the elevators and got close a couple of times at the door of the reception before the luncheon, but he never quite got within handshaking distance.

Willard Wirtz, the secretary of labor, was scheduled to come in but canceled at the last moment. That was a disappointment. I was going to try to make a big thing out of serving on the Labor Department's Commission on Employment Security, which had been created by the Social Security Act, although the principal beauty of serving had merely been to introduce me, with government travel vouchers, to the famous old Willard Hotel in Washington in its days of deepest decline. But a truly distinguished person did come in, and Ayres overlooked her. She was Patricia Roberts Harris, a young Washington attorney, bright and good-looking, who had made a name for herself in the civil rights movement. Unfortunately, all too many others also overlooked her through our fault. We depended on Bertha Moore, a local black leader and longtime good friend who was head of the Tea Time Study Club—an Akron institution—to make all the plans and bring out a crowd.

But it isn't always easy to corral a crowd. It turned out that Bertha needed help, and we didn't realize it in time. A very small audience heard a superb speaker. It is worth noting that of all the great people who came in for my campaign or at least during my campaign, including President Johnson, the next visitor, only one has been honored on a U.S. postage stamp. It is Patricia Roberts Harris (1925–1985), described by the U.S. Postal Service as "educator, lawyer, activist, diplomat, and advisor to presidents."

Nineteen **Up and Down**

Were all these events getting me any votes? The answer was yes. That doesn't mean I was winning, but, until late October, the people who were doing some polling—including Dr. Frank Simonetti of The University of Akron, a brilliant professor built like Alfred Hitchcock whose course in business finance I once took—told me the figures looked better all the time. I was aware, though, that I was appealing to a different constituency than had put me over the top when I used to run for the legislature. Back then, when only amorphous state issues were involved and Republican friends could vote for me as one of five in a field of ten, my strength came from the west side of Akron, in the predominantly Republican Fourth and Eighth Wards where I grew up, where my sister and I went to school, and where my mother was involved in all kinds of activities. She helped to start the hot lunch program and school uniforms at St. Sebastian's Church, as well as its annual flower show, and over the years she was president of organizations as varied as the Neighborhood Garden Club, St. Thomas Hospital's Linen Guild, and the Western Reserve Girl Scout Council.

In a campaign for Congress, however, party loyalties were the focus. That meant friends with Republican leanings were voting party, not friendship. For the first time, I needed strength in Democratic areas where I had never been strong—in Goodyear Heights, Firestone Park, Kenmore, and Barberton. That strength wasn't going to be easy to come by. Bill Ayres had cemented many personal loyalties in those areas over fourteen years with good staff services and popular votes on veterans' issues. Ayres was, moreover, the ranking Republican member of the House Veterans Affairs Committee, where he could continue to be helpful.

On the plus side, I had more support from labor unions than ever before. Some of the best help was coming from George Vasko, Ike Gold, Pooch (Francis) Maile, Ralph Smith, Beatrice Warwick, and Lucille Stevens of the Rubber Workers; from Lucy and Walter Mitchell of the Chemical Workers;

from Leo Dugan of the Labor Council; and from the building trades, steel-
workers, and communication workers.

I probably wasn't worrying as much as I should have about the shift in
support, because I was enjoying myself, and even indulging myself. For one
thing, Sam and Mary Ann Scherer, both very well-known artists and design-
ers, took me to their house one night and created a new image for me. My
hair was fluffed out, my lashes were lengthened, and my lips were made pos-
itively voluptuous for a photo portrait in which I emerged from Rem-
brandtesque shadows like the Queen of the Night. I was enough of a politician to know this was *not* the image I needed to project, but glamour was
new to me and irresistible. After the picture was put up on a billboard on
Broadway, I pulled up in front of St. Bernard's Church late one night, parked
my car, and unreservedly admired this darkling beauty with my name. True,
I did happen to notice that my name, printed in blue on a black background,
was hard to read, but oh well, I thought indulgently, nothing's perfect.

The 1964 "Rembrandt" Campaign
Photo.

Something else I remember with a smile was my one visit to Medina County. It was a wasted day as far as votes went—Medina County was a virtual desert for Democrats—but that day I brought my dog Cherry along to the County Fair, dressed in a white corduroy dog blanket a friend made for her with "Underdogs for McGovern" appliqued on it in red. I was a little sheepish about this, but Cherry stepped along proudly, and I was encouraged by the memory of Bill Ayres's son at a picnic years before wearing a similarly tasteful T-shirt proclaiming "Bill Ayres Is My Dad."

At the same time that I was enjoying myself, I was also creating new problems. Not blindly, but against all advice, I decided to speak out against a proposed constitutional amendment to permit prayer in public schools. The subject was as controversial then as it is now, and Ayres prudently said nothing on the subject, but for the very reason it was controversial I felt obliged to state my view. Virtually every organized religion, including Baptist, opposed the prayer amendment, but local Baptist leaders took a contrary view, believing anyone against the prayer amendment was against prayer itself. Among them was Dr. Dallas F. Billington, pastor of the Akron Baptist Temple, which was said to be the largest Baptist congregation in the world. Dr. Billington ominously said he would comment later on my position and did so, without a trace of Christian charity, in a sermon that was broadcast all over the district on the Sunday before the election.

Support for enactment of Medicare was far safer, in fact unexceptional for a Democrat, but it was anathema to Republicans in those days. There was nothing to gain from highlighting differences on the issue, but, of all the crazy things to do, I agreed to debate it before the Summit County Medical Society where, at most, one member in twenty favored it. I couldn't have had better coaches for the debate: Medicare was the topic of high school debating contests that year and two star debaters, Mark Skorman and Bill Shkurti, with shoe boxes full of cogent reference cards, primed me on the talking points and responses. I was thrilled to learn later that politics "took" with Bill. He became director of the Office of Budget and Management in

My 1964 visit to the Oval Office.

Governor Celeste's cabinet. (He is now a vice president of Ohio State University.) But when I got to the debate before a big crowd in an auditorium at Akron General Hospital, I found my opponent was a ringer from another Medical Society, not Bill Ayres, who was nowhere to be seen. I'm sure I won the debate that night, but it didn't do me a bit of good.

What was doing me good was President Johnson. In 1964, Lyndon Johnson was at the height of his popularity. We couldn't forget John Kennedy, but Johnson's style was so different it didn't invite comparison. He had already established his presidency on its own terms when he came to Akron in the fall campaign. I for one was running hopefully on his popularity with a picture of the two of us together, captioned "Great Team."

The picture had been taken in June in the Oval Office at the White House, and from all appearances we were having a pleasant conversation, seated side by side and shaking hands at Johnson's desk. The visit was really just a "photo opportunity" arranged for candidates for Congress that lasted only about half a minute before the next candidate was brought forward to sit for his half minute in the sun. That was time enough, however, to produce not only the photograph I was using but also a film clip nearly three minutes long, thanks to film shot from several angles at the same time and extended by a splendid view of the White House with flag flying.

I had more like half a day than half a minute with Johnson the next time I saw him on Wednesday, October 21, 1964. Johnson had been asked to speak at The University of Akron (Barry Goldwater had spoken there five days earlier), and Ernie Leonard, the Democratic county chairman, and I had both been cleared by the advance men to ride in the presidential limousine with President and Mrs. Johnson. The limousine was brought in before the presidential plane touched down at Akron-Canton Airport, and I was happily waiting beside it with an old friend, Phil Goulding, Washington correspondent for the *Cleveland Plain Dealer,* when Don Luffman, Mayor Erickson's political factotum, came over and told me that the mayor was going to ride in the limousine instead of me. It usually takes me a while to get angry, but not that time. I spoke up so hotly that Don fled and Phil turned away in disgust. I wondered for the first time what I was becoming. I also noticed for the first time what I probably should have noticed long before: my interests and the mayor's were not running on the same path. But those were only passing thoughts. Ernie and I were assigned to the two jump seats in the limousine, and it pulled forward as President Johnson and Lady Bird were getting off Air Force One.

All went well in the limousine until we began rolling up Interstate 77 toward Akron, and Johnson realized we had the road to ourselves. Interstate 77 was brand new at that time, and, while complete almost to the central interchange of the expressway in Akron, it was not yet open to traffic. That made it a perfect route for the president's safety. But it wasn't a perfect route for the president! Jack Valenti, his aide, since then the longtime president of the Motion Picture Association of America, was riding in the front seat with the driver and took the beating. His head went down between his shoulders, his ears were almost literally bent, as Johnson both expressed his extreme displeasure to find himself robbed of people and his suspicion—no, make that certainty—that Valenti had agreed to the route. At one lonely point, a man and a couple of children hung over a fence in an empty field beside the road. "Stop!" the president said. The driver apparently didn't hear and Valenti sat still lower in his seat.

Once in town, we couldn't avoid human beings, but they were scarce as we came in on South Main between the Goodrich plants on the west side of the street and the string of restaurants, bars, and pool halls on the other side. The only faces we saw were nervously looking out the plate glass store windows. Men with guns were stationed on the roofs.

But a huge crowd was waiting around Polsky's department store where we were going to turn up the hill to the university. The limousine was stopped by the crowd. In an instant, Johnson leaned over me, opened the door, and stepped out on to the running board. It was then I realized how important people were to him. His raincoat flapping around him, he reached down to the crowd, touching the fingertips of the people pressing forward around him. I watched with astonishment. It was as if he drew nourishment from them in great, satisfying draughts. At length, Lady Bird leaned across to pull at the hem of Johnson's raincoat, but contact with people was what he had been longing for, and he swatted her hand aside. Finally, the security people cleared the area around the car, and we moved on. Johnson settled back into his seat with a deep sigh of fulfillment. Not a word had been spoken.

At Memorial Hall, where the president was to speak at the university, we came in through a phalanx of security personnel to the platform where Dr. Norman P. Auburn, the president of the university, Ed Erickson, the mayor of Akron, and others were already seated in front of an enthusiastic crowd. Given an opportunity to speak, I delightedly gave an old-fashioned

President Johnson's 1964 visit to The University of Akron. *Seated L to R:* Dr. Norman P. Auburn, President, The University of Akron, Lady Bird, Ed Erickson, Mayor of Akron, Ike Gold (back row), me.

"man who" speech for the first time in my life. Ernie Leonard was to introduce Johnson, so I couldn't end up "giving" the audience the president of the United States in the best "man who" form, but I came so close to doing so that Johnson half rose, not altogether sure for a moment that someone else was going to be introducing him.

Not least of the privileges of being on the platform with Johnson was that I could read his TelePrompTers. I don't know whom I admired more—the president for his stirring speech, which frequently departed from the text, or whoever was trying to position returns to the TelePrompTer. I could see the text scrolling up and down as someone desperately sought to offer new beginning points. Johnson was so smooth, however, and the TelePrompTer so responsive that the audience never knew he was in and out of his prepared remarks over and over again.

The day wasn't over yet. Back in the limousine, heading for the ramp to the expressway, Johnson suddenly asked Ernie and me if we knew the way to the *Akron Beacon Journal.* Of course we did, and he told us to tell the driver how to get there. The driver had to turn around suddenly on Carroll Street, six or seven blocks from the *Beacon,* and head for Exchange Street. So, too, did the police escorts, much to their surprise. The first car or two was already lost heading south on the expressway. The others turned themselves inside out with brakes squealing and sirens dropping to low moans. Johnson must have made some unannounced prearrangement with John S. Knight, the publisher of the *Akron Beacon Journal,* because he seemed to expect Knight to be in the office, and Valenti may also have phoned ahead from the limousine, because when we got to the *Akron Beacon Journal,* a small crowd already knew he was coming and was packed in the lobby. Johnson went up to Knight's office on the elevator, but it wasn't long before he was back and Knight with him, all smiles, to send him on his way. About then, Johnson, seeing me, remembered he maybe had a local obligation, and he took my arm. "Take care of this little girl," he told Knight. I think I laughed. I hope I did.

The *Akron Beacon Journal*'s endorsement was sure to go to Ayres. The paper had been supporting him for seven terms, and there was no compelling reason to change its view. But I hoped I would be treated gently, having been generously, if anything overgenerously, endorsed every time I ran for the legislature, and supported with kind words when I was appointed to the Public Utilities Commission, when I resigned from it, and when I received various honors. When the time came, the *Beacon* endorsed Ayres, as expected, because of his long service and the future value of his senior position. But, as for me, in words I didn't save and chose to forget, the implication was that I had reached beyond my capacity. Mentally, I railed at this. Didn't anyone remember that I was the only House member unanimously voted Outstanding House Member by newspapermen covering the General Assembly in my last term? Didn't the *Beacon* remember its own praises? But "Always forward," Clarence Motz used to say.

I had the election-night party at my house, borrowing chairs everywhere and buying dozens of glasses at the Miracle Mart. Cherry wore her special dog blanket, and we had a pretty good time, but it was evident early that I was losing. On the final count, I got just under 47 percent of the vote and Ayres got 53 percent.

Of course, I wished I had come closer, for those who helped me as well as for myself. But I had had a grand run.

A fifteen-year run, one could say, if one counted from those first days above the Backstage Bar. Fifteen really great years. But when I looked at a future in politics, I saw nothing as satisfying to come. It was time to set a new course.

Epilogue

Did I miss being in politics? Of course I did. I lost touch with many friends. I missed the excitement of winning and even the grief of losing. I missed the thrill of participating in great events and the good feeling that came from solving problems. Most of all, and for the longest time, I missed the sense of purpose politics had brought me.

But it was nice to have time on my hands. I hardly knew what to do with it for awhile. And one thing I didn't miss was having my motives questioned if I didn't vote the way someone thought I should, or whenever I got interested in some obscure issue. Then is when I was very much aware that most people who aren't in politics considered politics a dirty business. If they liked me anyway, it was because they thought I was different.

I wasn't different, and I was proud to be a politician. For the same reason I used to answer "blue" when asked "color of dog" on my Kerry blue terrier's annual license application, I enjoyed responding "politician" when asked for my occupation on questionnaires. Not only was it true, but it upset expectations, and that's always fun to do. Politics was often fun. I enjoyed laughing over crazy happenings and human foibles. I enjoyed gossip, rumors, and speculating on outcomes. It made me feel good to surprise people with unexpected service and occasional insights. It made me feel powerful to have inside information.

All these good things about politics depended on winning elections more often than losing, and winning, moreover, an office I liked that paid a living wage. Some people like being councilmen, mayors, sheriffs, judges, or clerks of court. But none of the offices that might have been within my reach in 1964 appealed to me the way Congress had or as much as the legislature and the Public Utilities Commission once did.

Fortunately, I still liked being a lawyer, and, within the scope of that profession, I liked public utility law best of all and the logic and symmetry of utility regulation back when it was real regulation. I was already specializing in that field after I returned from Columbus, but if it hadn't have been for a retainer from the city of Akron for some work on utility issues, I would have had a hard time limiting my practice to that somewhat narrow field. That's why, when Ohio Edison Company asked me to join its legal department after the election in 1964, I did so without any particular agonizing over the decision. I was heading for work I already knew I would like.

It was the right choice. I liked the work. I liked the people I was working with. And, as an old politician, I enjoyed being encouraged to continue my involvement in community activities, including serving on boards and committees, almost without number. I even ran for election in 1969 as a member of Summit County's first county charter commission—a nonpartisan, unpaid position—and read the returns with the same old excitement, thrilled to come in first again after years out of the mainstream. When the return address of the Board of Elections on the commission's charter proposals being mailed to voters in 1970 was found to be impermissible, Ohio Edison opened up its auditorium and kitchen for the more than one hundred volunteers who were occupied for several days blanking out the return address on over 200,000 pieces retrieved from the post office. Not many companies would offer that kind of support.

What kept surprising me year after year, however, was that women from Summit County were no longer running for the legislature. Surely other women realized it offered not only extraordinary opportunities to be of service but also a chance to showcase their abilities. My own years in politics were not only immensely satisfying, they opened many doors for me at the time and have continued to do so all these years since. But thirty years went by with no woman in the legislature from Summit County, a period when women were otherwise striving to establish themselves.

At first I thought this was because promising young women, having been caught up in the new movement for liberation, were so determined to be aggrieved by discrimination that they refused to take even the well-proven paths to success. I later realized that was unfair, however. Apparently what happened is that after only a few years went by without a woman from Summit in the legislature, the history of past elections was so completely forgotten that women didn't think of running or didn't know they could win.

Betty Sutton was one who didn't know the old history. After she and Karen Doty were both elected to the legislature from Summit County in 1992, Betty remarked at a meeting I attended that I was the first woman to serve in the legislature from Summit County. I hastened to say I was *not* the first. The first was Anna F. O'Neil, first elected in 1932, who served in the House for twenty years and held the powerful position of chairman of the House Finance Committee for a time. Next, Blanche Hower was elected in 1934, and Catherine Dobbs and Sophia Harter joined Anna O'Neil in the legislature in 1949—Catherine in the Senate and Sophia in the House. That made me the fifth, not the first, when I was elected in 1954. Then Betty Smith, elected in 1958, and Mary McGowan, elected in 1960, were sixth and seventh. Karen Doty and Betty Sutton became eighth and ninth. Twyla Roman and Barbara Sykes are now tenth and eleventh.

Nowadays I'm surprised by a very different political phenomenon: women here are being elected as judges at every level, including the Ohio Supreme Court, where Deborah Cook has made a name for herself. With gender now only an incidental consideration, political office is at last, as it should be, open to all with the inclination to run and the personal circumstances that permit it. Term limits are discouraging, and so is the need to raise huge sums of money for some campaigns, but the thrills and the satisfactions are still there, awaiting anyone who can make it through to election.

Running for office is worth the effort, if only for the experience. My own experience was almost too good to be true, and my memories of politics are richly peopled. I still have three friends I met first when I was working at the campaign headquarters above the Backstage Bar more than fifty years ago— John Stadler, Bernie Rosen, and Bill Victor. I remember hundreds more, possibly thousands, from all the years that followed. Mention to me a town in Ohio—Celina, Wauseon, Ironton, Wilmington, Sugar Creek—and a friend from legislative days will come to mind. Recall to me an old event and

I can bring back the people in it. When I remember church basements, union halls, clubhouses, and ballrooms, I see the faces there.

And places. I can sit down now at Ray Potts's coffee counter in the basement of the courthouse. I can pass out cards and matches at dawn at the back gate to Goodrich over the old canal. I can walk into Tomsik's Park and see the picnics spread out and the food on the grills. I can sit again at my desk in the front row of the Ohio House of Representatives and find the Cuyahoga County members around me. I can eat breakfast once more with an old friend in the Victorian Room of the Deshler-Hilton Hotel. Who says these places are all gone now! They are still there for me.

Old habits and outlooks have persisted too, but that isn't always good. For one thing, I am still offering opinions on all kinds of public issues—even things I don't know anything about. For another, back when I was in politics, I quit even trying to rely on my memory for plans, and to this day, after being relatively idle for years, I still depend totally on a pocket calendar. If I forget to write down a date or write a wrong date, there is no self-correcting mechanism. That sometimes means I don't show up when I should. Once I cooked dinner for eight a night too soon. That was pretty bad. It wasn't the kind of dinner one could warm up the next night.

In enlightened self-interest, I acquired a few virtues in politics. I said yes whenever I was asked for help, even before I knew what for. If I gave my word, I kept it like a vow. If someone did me a favor, I knew I owed a favor in return. I was totally loyal to political allies, although I always had friends across the aisle. I never said anything bad about anyone, because whatever I said might be repeated. I didn't even agree when someone else said something bad, because whatever it was might be given as my opinion.

I'm sorry to say I haven't always practiced the political virtues since I got out of politics. Apparently, however, they are just under the surface. Not too long ago I was ready to snap at a clerk who was very unhelpful. I stopped short, thinking, as I always used to do, that he might be a voter. I had to laugh to myself then. Despite all my years out of politics, I am still a politician!

Illustration Credits

Page 6, Photo by Harris & Ewing at O'Neil's; author's collection.

Page 8, Author's collection.

Page 11, Author's collection.

Page 12, Author's collection.

Page 21, Author's collection.

Page 30, Author's collection.

Page 34, Author's collection.

Page 40, Author's collection.

Page 43, Photo by Frances Murphy; reprinted with permission of the *Akron Beacon Journal.*

Page 45, Author's collection.

Page 46, Author's collection.

Page 66, Author's collection.

Page 68, Author's collection.

Page 70, Author's collection.

Page 76, Courtesy AP/ World Wide Photos.

Page 77, Courtesy of the Ohio Trucking Association.

Page 90, Cartoon by Eugene Craig; courtesy of the *Columbus Dispatch.*

Page 94, Courtesy of the Ohio Democratic Party.

Page 110, Photo by C. J. Ewald; courtesy of Cinergy Services, Inc.

Page 111, Reprinted with permission of the *Akron Beacon Journal.*

Page 118, Author's collection.

Page 120, Reprinted with permission of the *Akron Beacon Journal.*

Page 121, Courtesy of Fred Tambling Studio.

Page 128, Photo by Dale Smith; author's collection.

Page 134, LBJ Library Photo by Robert L. Knudsen.

Page 138, LBJ Library Photo by Robert L. Knudsen.

Page 144, Author's collection.

Page 146, Author's collection.

Page 149, The University of Akron Archives.

Index

Series on Ohio History and Culture

John H. White and Robert J. White, Sr., *The Island Queen: Cincinnati's Excursion Steamer*

H. Roger Grant, *Ohio's Railway Age in Postcards*

Frances McGovern, *Written on the Hills: The Making of the Akron Landscape*

Keith McClellan, *The Sunday Game: At the Dawn of Professional Football*

Steve Love and David Giffels, *Wheels of Fortune: The Story of Rubber in Akron*

Alfred Winslow Jones, *Life, Liberty, and Property: A Story of Conflict and a Measurement of Conflicting Rights*

David Brendan Hopes, *A Childhood in the Milky Way: Becoming a Poet in Ohio*

John Keim, *Legends by the Lake: The Cleveland Browns at Municipal Stadium*

Richard B. Schwartz, *The Biggest City in America: A Fifties Boyhood in Ohio*

Tom Rumer, *Unearthing the Land: The Story of Ohio's Scioto Marsh*

Ian Adams, Barney Taxel, and Steve Love, *Stan Hywet Hall and Gardens*

William F. Romain, *Mysteries of the Hopewell: Astronomers, Geometers, and Magicians of the Eastern Woodlands*

Dale Topping, edited by Eric Brothers, *When Giants Roamed the Sky: Karl Arnstein and the Rise of Airships from Zeppelin to Goodyear*

Millard F. Rogers, Jr., *Rich in Good Works: Mary M. Emery of Cincinnati*

Frances McGovern, *Fun, Cheap, and Easy: My Life in Ohio Politics, 1949–1964*

Larry Nelson, editor, *A History of Jonathan Alder: His Captivity and Life with the Indians*

About the Author

Frances McGovern, a lawyer now retired from the Ohio Edison Company, has served her native city of Akron in many capacities. Active in politics and community affairs, she was a three-term member of the Ohio House of Representatives, chair of the Ohio Public Utilities Commission, member of The University of Akron Board of Trustees, and president of the United Way of Summit County. She is also the author of *Written on the Hills: The Making of the Akron Landscape.*

About the Book

Fun, Cheap, and Easy: My Life in Ohio Politics, 1949–1964 was designed and typeset by Kachergis Book Design of Pittsboro, North Carolina. The typeface, StonePrint, was designed by Sumner Stone in 1991.

Fun, Cheap, and Easy: My Life in Ohio Politics, 1949–1964 was printed on 60-pound Writers Offset Natural and bound by Thomson-Shore, Inc., of Dexter, Michigan.